Bible

Interpretations

Eighth Series
April 2-June 25, 1893

Matthew, Job, Proverbs, Ezekiel, and Malachi

Bible Interpretations

Eighth Series

Matthew, Job, Proverbs, Ezekiel, and Malachi

These Bible Interpretations were given during the early eighteen nineties at the Christian Science Theological Seminary at Chicago, Illinois. This Seminary was independent of the First Church of Christ Scientist in Boston, Mass.

By

Emma Curtis Hopkins

President of the Christian Science Theological Seminary at Chicago, Illinois

WISEWOMAN PRESS

Bible Interpretations: Eighth Series

By Emma Curtis Hopkins

© WiseWoman Press

Managing Editor: Michael Terranova

ISBN: 978-0945385-58-5

WiseWoman Press

Vancouver, WA 98665

www.wisewomanpress.com

www.emmacurtishopkins.com

CONTENTS

Editors Note

All lessons starting with the Seventh Series of Bible Interpretations will be Sunday postings from the Inter-Ocean Newspaper in Chicago, Illinois. Many of the lessons in the following series were retrieved from the International New Thought Association Archives, in Mesa, Arizona by, Rev Joanna Rogers. Many others were retrieved from libraries in Chicago, and the Library of Congress, by Rev. Natalie Jean.

All the lessons follow the Sunday School Lesson Plan published in "Peloubet's International Sunday School Lessons". The passages to be studied are selected by an International Committee of traditional Bible Scholars.

Some of the Emma's lessons don't have a title. In these cases the heading will say "Comments and Explanations of the Golden Text," followed by the Bible passages to be studied.

Foreword

By Rev. Natalie R. Jean

I have read many teachings by Emma Curtis Hopkins, but the teachings that touch the very essence of my soul are her Bible Interpretations. There are many books written on the teachings of the Bible, but none can touch the surface of the true messages more than these Bible interpretations. With each word you can feel and see how Spirit spoke through Emma. The mystical interpretations take you on a wonderful journey to Self Realization.

Each passage opens your consciousness to a new awareness of the realities of life. The illusions of life seem to disappear through each interpretation. Emma teaches that we are the key that unlocks the doorway to the light that shines within. She incorporates ideals of other religions into her teachings, in order to understand the commonalities, so that there is a complete understanding of our Oneness. Emma opens our eyes and mind to a better today and exciting future.

Emma Curtis Hopkins, one of the Founders of New Thought teaches us to love ourselves, to speak our Truth, and to focus on our Good. My life has moved in wonderful directions because of her teachings. I know the only thing that can move me in this world is God. May these interpretations guide you to a similar path and may you truly remember that "There Is Good For You and You Ought to Have It."

Introduction

Emma Curtis Hopkins was born in 1849 in Killingsly, Connecticut. She passed on April 8, 1925. Mrs. Hopkins had a marvelous education and could read many of the worlds classical texts in their original language. During her extensive studies she was always able to discover the Universal Truths in each of the world's sacred traditions. She quotes from many of these teachings in her writings. As she was a very private person, we know little about her personal life. What we do know has been gleaned from other people or from the archived writings we have been able to discover.

Emma Curtis Hopkins was one of the greatest influences on the New Thought movement in the United States. She taught over 50,000 people the Universal Truth of knowing "God is All there is." She taught many of founders of early New Thought, and in turn these individuals expanded the influence of her teachings. All of her writings encourage the student to enter into a personal relationship with God. She presses us to deny anything except the Truth of this spiritual Presence in every area of our lives. This is the central focus of all her teachings.

The first six series of Bible Interpretations were presented at her seminary in Chicago, Illinois. The remaining Series', probably close to thirty, were printed in the Inter Ocean Newspaper in Chicago. Many of the lessons are no longer available for various reasons. It is the intention of WiseWoman Press to publish as many of these Bible Interpretations as possible. Our hope is that any missing lessons will be found or directed to us.

I am very honored to join the long line of people that have been involved in publishing Emma Curtis Hopkins's Bible Interpretations. Some confusion exists as to the numbering sequence of the lessons. In the early 1920's many of the lessons were published by the Highwatch Fellowship. Inadvertently the first two lessons were omitted from the numbering system. Rev. Joanna Rogers has corrected this mistake by finding the first two lessons and restoring them to their rightful place in the order. Rev. Rogers has been able to find many of the missing lessons at the International New Thought Alliance archives in Mesa, Arizona. Rev. Rogers painstakingly scoured the archives for the missing lessons as well as for Mrs. Hopkins other works. She has published much of what was discovered. WiseWoman Press is now publishing the correctly numbered series of the Bible Interpretations.

In the early 1940's, there was a resurgence of interest in Emma's works. At that time, Highwatch Fellowship began to publish many of her writings, and it was then that *High Mysticism*, her seminal work was published. Previously, the material contained in High Mysticism was only available as individual lessons and was brought together in book form for the first time. Although there were many errors in these first publications and many Bible verses were incorrectly quoted, I am happy to announce that WiseWoman Press is now publishing *High Mysticism* in the a corrected format. This corrected form was scanned faithfully from the original, individual lessons.

The next person to publish some of the Bible Lessons was Rev. Marge Flotron from the Ministry of Truth International in Chicago, Illinois. She published the Bible Lessons as well as many of Emma's other works. By her initiative, Emma's writings were brought to a larger audience when DeVorss & Company, a longtime publisher of Truth Teachings, took on the publication of her key works.

In addition, Dr. Carmelita Trowbridge, founding minister of The Sanctuary of Truth in Alhambra, California, inspired her assistant minister, Rev. Shirley Lawrence, to publish many of Emma's works, including the first three series of Bible Interpretations. Rev. Lawrence created mail order courses for many of these Series. She has graciously passed on any information she had, in order to assure that these works continue to inspire individuals and groups who are called to further study of the teachings of Mrs. Hopkins.

Finally, a very special acknowledgement goes to Rev Natalie Jean, who has worked diligently to retrieve several of Emma's lessons from the Library of Congress, as well as libraries in Chicago. Rev. Jean hand-typed many of the lessons she found on microfilm. Much of what she found is on her website, www.highwatch.net.

It is with a grateful heart that I am able to pass on these wonderful teachings. I have been studying dear Emma's works for fifteen years. I was introduced to her writings by my mentor and teacher, Rev. Marcia Sutton. I have been overjoyed with the results of delving deeply into these Truth Teachings.

In 2004, I wrote a Sacred Covenant entitled "Resurrecting Emma," and created a website, www.emmacurtishopkins.com. The result of creating this covenant and website has brought many of Emma's works into my hands and has deepened my faith in God. As a result of my love for these works, I was led to become a member of Wise-Woman Press and to publish these wonderful teachings. God is Good.

My understanding of Truth from these divinely inspired teachings keeps bringing great Joy, Freedom, and Peace to my life.

Dear reader; It is with an open heart that I offer these works to you, and I know they will touch you as they have touched me. Together we are living in the Truth that God is truly present, and living for and through each of us.

The greatest Truth Emma presented to us is "My Good is my God, Omnipresent, Omnipotent and Omniscient."

Rev. Michael Terranova

WiseWoman Press

Vancouver, Washington, 2010

LESSON I

RESURRECTION OF CHRIST

Matthew 28:1-10

One Indestructible

There is one indestructible substance pervading all things from the remotest star to the nearest dust particle. This substance is finer than any substance cognized by the senses. It is finer than the attraction of gravitation, cohesion, disintegration. It can only be cognized by the mind. It can only be handled by the thoughts of the mind. And only the understanding power of the mind can make it useful.

He who by any manner of thinking handles this substance and realizes that its nature is his nature soon finds himself experiencing vital renewals throughout body and mind. He has begun the "animation of the particular from the universal," an art earnestly sought after by the ancients.

If he shall ever enter into an understanding of what thoughts are invariably certain to revitalize

1

his being he will see that, though the temple be destroyed, yet in three days can he raise it again. He will see what Jesus Christ meant by all mankind's being of the same family with himself, having the same Father and gifted with the same abilities. The resurrection will be to Him no miracle. That the beauty of the all-pervading substance must break out here or there, in rose or infant, because of its having been molded by beautiful thoughts; that the wisdom of the all-pervading substance must break out here and there by reason of having been handled by true thoughts, will be to him as easy to demonstrate as that the angles of a triangle are two right angles. He will realize literally, *"I am in the Father, and ye in Me, and I in you."* He will know this substance perfectly, and knowing it will be eternal life for him.

"And this eternal life, that they might know Thee the only true God, and Jesus Christ whom Thou hast sent."

Life In Eternal Abundance

He will see that if beauty breaks forth here and there because of the here and there activities that produce beauty, and now he can himself act in the way to manifest beauty wheresoever he will, that all things and all people may as well exhibit the beauty of the willing waiting principle as for only a few to be beautiful. If he finds the activities within his own nature which by using he can bring forth music by voice or instrument, and he sees that everything and everybody might surpass the symphonies and sonatas of the great masters through understanding the substance which is divine harmony itself, he will not drill with voice or instrument to bring forth the songs of Zion, but will finger the chords of the everlasting spirit of harmony stretched in infinite number every object on earth and in heaven. The substance that holds the worlds in its breath is life itself. He who understands it has life in eternal abundance. It is wisdom itself. He who understands it knows all things. Nothing is hidden from him. He laughs at death. *"Though after my skin worms destroy this body, yet in my flesh shall I see God."* He is removed from the fear of senility. The secret of perpetual light is his.

The resurrection of Jesus Christ was the necessitous result of his understanding of the all-pervading substance. Whoever understands this substance must roll away the stones from his tomb, must ascend out of his grave bodily, must be indestructible being because he has drunk his full of indestructible fluid, he has eaten his full of imperishable bread. Having once risen from the tomb, he may or may not appear substantially present to mankind. Jesus Christ does not choose to appear often in our time as he appeared shortly after the apparent crucifixion, but he can thus come there is no doubt, for whoever has learned the way he taught, most nearly to his knowledge thereof, has most nearly touched his miracle working.

The twenty eighth chapter of Matthew, first to tenth verses, describes the belief of the Christian world in the potency of the universal substance as a revival to the body and mind in defiance of the worst possible efforts against its action. Jesus Christ had said that "The Father" was not ready for Him to make the test at one time, and He slipped through the multitude and escaped from them that He might bring more fully unto Himself the quickening principle. He had been thirty years working with it by means of thoughts untaught in the schools and churches of His time before He wrought a miracle. Then at Cana of Galilee, He turned water into wine. After three years of working outward demonstrations of dealing with the mysterious and unknown substance He was ready to demonstrate that full and perfect life for every faculty would waken after a necessary period in every human being; within three days if as fully in the understanding of the life substance as he was; within longer periods if not as fully in the understanding. He knew He had solved the problem of the ages.

The Resurrection

There was in His friends no full faith in His ability to rise from so covered a grave. Yet so gloriously did He demonstrate it that His very thoughts formulated angels with countenances radiant in light and penetrating as lightning and forms clothed in dazzling white raiment. His very thoughts were alive and glistening. The two

Mary's sought for His closed sepulchre. His nearest friends mourned His unrisen body. But He was alive and in Galilee. Galilee means circuit. All the places chosen by Him were significant of the demonstration He made at each one. He closed the circuit of His minority at Galilee. He closed the disciples' belief in poverty and disgrace at Galilee. He closed the circuit of their doubt of His power on a mountain in Galilee.

With His demonstration of the ability of a doctrine to feed the being of man He proved that nothing is too small to express all the beauty, the joy, the light of the universal principle. He explained how nobody is too ignorant to know all things without the necessity of a well-developed intellect. By the exercise of the intellect, intellect fails. By the right draught upon the all-pervading substance intelligence is intensified with unlimited possibilities to infinite wisdom.

By His rising from the sepulchre after a seeming of crucifixion He brought the circuit of man's belief in the power of death to a close for whosoever would accept His instructions. He showed that the fine force that pervades the planets, being itself consciousness whoever breathes it by that process of believing in it suggested by Him must have life in all its manifestations fully energized in himself.

It is conscious hearing in itself; therefore thinks about this fine vital elixir in the right way must make a draught upon it which reanimates the life of the hearing faculty in man infinitely. Jesus unstopped deaf ears by the life force he radiated wherever he walked, as a consequence of his understanding the fine life of the inner ears. "He unstopped deaf ears," He did more and further than that. He caused the ears to hear angelic voices giving explicit direction, which way to walk to find the satisfied life.

The fine force is the conscious skill of demonstration in itself; therefore, whoever thinks directly toward it instead, of toward instruments and methods must make a draught upon it for deftness and conscious skill in bringing to pass good works of whatever kind he chooses.

It is conscious ownership of all things, and therefore whoever looks straight to it for his provisions must, if looking by the understanding of his mind and not by his physical endeavors, find that he makes a draught upon it for plenty. He cannot help bringing his sustenance from it when he understands it as sustenance any more than he can help coming forth from ignorance by handling the fine fluid thereof with those thoughts that make a draught upon it for wisdom.

It is light itself in pure consciousness. Whoever came near Jesus Christ felt the reanimation of His sight by the conscious seeing, radiated by His mind. By a process He made clear to His disciples. He made a draught upon the universal principle, which is conscious seeing, and He healed every blindness by His radiation of the seeing mind with which He had stored himself. He called it the Father sometimes. He called, it God sometimes. He called it Lord and Holy Spirit.

He found in this universal essential all good in conscious readiness. He gave all the years of his human travel to practicing with it, leaving entirely out of his interest the methods of men. "Your fathers did eat manna and are dead," He said, *"I have a bread which if a man eat thereof he shall never die".* Then they thought He meant material bread, but He said matter profiteth nothing.

Shakes Nature Herself

This lesson shows how the sight of Him and the hearing of Him for three years without practicing the instructions He gave brought the continued sight and hearing of Him. It shows the effect upon the world which opposition to the life, necessitously set going by the understanding of life, itself brings, "There was an earthquake."Opposition to the action of this energy shakes nature herself.

Jesus Christ by his coming forth unharmed from material injuries brought to light the immortality of all the powers of mankind. He had already taught that one virtue in a man is one unconscious feeding upon eternal substance that will by and by permeate and quicken all the other virtues. *"A little leaven leaveneth the whole lump."* Thus one virtue, though it seems not to save the life of man, will by reason of its irresistible life, here or there, today or tomorrow, "raise him a glorious body." Many virtues raise him promptly.

All the virtues keep him forever raised out of the reach of death, out of the reach of loss, out of the reach of feebleness, out of the reach of ignorance. A virtue is only a right handling of the wondrous pervading substance.

The glory of Jesus Christ was that, having all the virtues through drawing rightly upon all the life of the universe, He took each man's estate and explained unto him separately how, through all time, he should proceed to have more abundant life by exercise of his nearest talent. As nearly as we can catch the words of His law of life, He meant for us to ignore the claim of evil by making wise draughts upon the full good in this universal presence. He would have us ignore burdens and drudges by breathing in large draughts of the everywhere pervading consciousness of freedom. He would have us ignore poverty and loss by turning our faces toward the consciousness of ownership, which being once felt as present soon potentialities every faculty of him that recognizes its presence.

There was no good, which he did not draw from the fine breath which, when caught consciously, man becomes alive with. The man who molds the vital ethers of omnipresence by right thoughts about its bounty brings forth bountifully. He need not sow seeds into arable soil to fruit in corn and wheat in a far-off autumn time. He handles those plants and trees which were created before their slow shadows were flung into seed time for harvest summer and winter. Jesus Christ ignored every process of creation and brought into sight those things which He pleased, not by skill in quick operations with material things, but by understanding that back of the material things lies the substance that waits to be molded into manifestation, through forms, or independent of forms. The loaves that He wrought out of the spirit were not stones or wood made eatable according to the wishes of Satan, but were repetitious of the five loaves at hand. The angel who spoke to the women was not an inspired man, but the formulation of one of His masterful thoughts as it swiftly gathered out of the first cause of all things its glistening beauty.

But He did not disdain to inspire forms with new qualities, new potencies. The water at the wedding feast was inspired with red wine. The apostles on the day of Pentecost were inspired to speak with new tongues. Thus it is not the destruction of forms but the inspiration of forms which understanding of the nature of this everywhere-present substance gives. Everything quickens with the wine of gladness, which will suit it best. "Come, buy wine and milk without money and without price," that ye may live anew. The poor having this gospel preached unto them are inspired with plenty and so the resurrection of the universal ether in them comes as substance.

Gospel To The Poor

Prophecy had said that the Messiah's words should be a gospel to the poor. Whoever understands this substance molds it wisely into bounty for all men, instead of leaving millions in squalor through not understanding how to feed every one.

Knowing this law of action, nobody is poor. All the plenty with which certain men are provided has come to them through the right use of the origin of bounty which somebody unknowingly made. Close attention to the origin of bounty reveals its readiness to bless all creatures alike.

The substance which is the primal essential out of which all things are fashioned yields itself utterly to thoughts. The fingers cannot handle it. The eyes cannot see it. The thoughts make of it what it names.

If a man's thoughts choose to proclaim that he is unfortunate he makes misfortune manifest. If he chooses to mold, the fine substance with gracious praises of his rightful inheritance of good he cannot help rising, filled with the good he has praised. If the lack of Judgment besets a man he has only to reanimate his mind with touching the life stuff that is judgment itself. The touch thereof is life. He will gather to himself large draughts of the mind on which his judgment can revive, and the judgment within him being fed by the judgment without him, comes forth from its tomb. This is resurrection, as demonstrated by Jesus. The life stuff of which His being inhaled to infinite over-flowing was the Christ. All who learn the way of life that he taught, so that every faculty is revived out of its hiding sepulchre, are Christ also. For that which is universal good is Christ. They who expand all their inherent powers to infinite over-flowing are Christ resurrected again, as in Jesus. It is no miracle. It is law.

The life stuff pervading all things now, may now be manifested in all things, as infinite life, infinite health, infinite strength of any faculty. Who is there with understanding of how to resur-rect or revive all things now from the substance whose name is not the past or the future, but Now? Though you do know how to mold a measure of health out of this presence by your thoughts, do you know how to think into it and around it with thoughts that revive every department of being now?

As its name is Life so its name is Now. What-ever Jesus did He did at once, because He fed His innate love of the present with the substance that can revive your love of the present into fulfillment. Before the Marys arrived He had already risen. This is the way of the Now.

There is no law of resurrection from death ex-cept by the revival of the deathless germs of faculty hidden in the tomb of non-usage.

When you touch the fine pervading influence of the world with the thoughts which will spring up from thinking over this fact of existence it shall come to pass that "while ye are yet speaking I will answer, and before ye can call I will hear" for this substance is named the visibility of God while we are speaking.

Inter-Ocean Newspaper, April 2, 1893

LESSON II

UNIVERSAL ENERGY

Book of Job, Part I

A very well-known and successful physician told of a case he had under his care, far gone in consumption and utterly incurable from a medical standpoint. The patient went to her priest and he gave her a bottle of the water of Lourdes to drink. The doctor did not relate how many bottles of the water her priest administered, but he was willing to testify that the case he had understood to be hopeless had bloomed into a healthy woman with not the slightest symptoms of illness of any sort.

Repeating this story to a medical specialist, he said he could not well believe that the faith nature of even a consumptive might be roused to the pitch of actual cure. A lady asked the specialist why, if the faith nature in man is so capable when roused, it were not more wise to study the successful mode of stimulative faith in would-be doctors than to spend so much time and energy of mind on quinine, honey bees' sting, Spanish flies, etc. He

13

replied that what one man would have faith in would not appeal to the faith function of another man. One would easily believe in the bones of St. Anthony; another could not be healed by those bones, but would throw down his crutches at the sight of a picture of the Virgin Mary, which not arousing the healing faith of a third, he must believe on Jesus Christ, and so on, till what to instruct a man to have faith in would become impossible, there being so many different objects and so many different natures in mankind.

The questioner persisted that, even so, each believer believed in his object as charged by one and the same power, viz., God, so that finally it all amounted to the same faith. "Do you not think it shows that there is a unity of feeling in the race mind as to what power it is to which to attribute cure? Even doctors think that God has invested minerals and insects with a portion of His own healing energy, so that it is upon a moiety (one of two equal parts) of divine energy, and not upon universal and divine energy, they are drawing for accomplishing their cures when using nature's items. Do you not believe that if they would learn to draw from the universal energy for their healing principles they might succeed where now they fail?" The learned doctor shook his head and said that faith in Power itself could not be learned; it was out of the reach of human beings. All who had attempted to cast themselves into the unknowable universal had floundered round in the mazes of impossible mysticisms and amounted finally to nothing.

Job is the example of one who turned his mind utterly away from its natural bearing upon the external and tangible to unassisted and unbe- friended trust in Power itself. Jesus had faith in power itself, and handled objective phenomena not as His instructors but as His servants. There are multitudes of examples of people who have found material things inadequate to restore unto them health, life, prosperity and, pushed to ex- tremities, have found the Universal Being quite adequate. Does it seem at all strange to any- body that it might be the height of wisdom to learn our human relation to power itself? How do we know but that we might never arrive at extremi- ties if we understood the "unknowable universal"? Who tells us that the One Power who is the abso- lutely capable, is the principle, which it is folly to investigate? Is it Jesus? Is it Job? As our lesson is Job (Verses 17-27), let us hear him: *"Surely I would speak to the Almighty, and I desire to reason with God"* (Job 13:3) — for *"ye are all physicians of no value"* (Job 13:4).

What was the result? He testified to getting face to face with the Absolute: *"I have heard of Thee by the hearing of the ear, but now mine eye seeth Thee"* (Job 42:5).

And after seeing the Great Being face to face, what? *"The Lord turned the captivity of Job* (Job

15

42:10) ... *and blessed the latter end of Job more than his beginning"* (Job 42:12).

It is almost universally conceded now that Job was a real character of patriarchal times. His home was at Uz, on the east of the Jordan. He was a morally blameless man, generous, religious, peaceable. All at once, calamity followed calamity. The Sabeans from the Southwest and the Chaldeans from the Northeast destroyed his cattle and his camels. A cyclone from the desert, with lightning and whirlwinds, struck down his house and all his children perished. Last of all, a most loathsome malady attacked his body.

Formerly, he believed in the same God his friends described. Their idea of the Universal Absolute was the same as his idea, but when all these calamities struck him, he saw he had been depending upon his idea of Deity instead of upon Deity itself. He saw that it was just as unreliable action of mind to rely upon its idea of power as to rely upon material symbols of power. So he turned his soul away utterly from all that he had believed and seen, to what was above and beyond and independent of all, yet responsible for all. His struggle out of the net of his past ideas was almost superhuman. *"Behold I go forward, but He is not there, and backward, but I cannot perceive Him"* (Job 23:8). *"But He is of One Mind and who can turn Him?"* (Job 23:13)

Job finally found one idea of his own mind that was the only thing that hid him from the passover he was seeking. It was the idea of righteousness in self as separate from the one righteousness. He learned that all goodness is one goodness; all mind one mind, whether in the convict or the saint. He had been thinking with his friends that there were circles of necessity fixed for man. He had been thinking there were things too high for him to meddle with. He had doubtless thought with the renowned specialist that it was dangerous to plunge past the known into the abysmal unknown from whence, without doubt, all good is derived.

He was a living witness to the proclamation of James that *"Whosoever shall keep the whole law and yet offend in one point, he is guilty of all."* (James 2:10). For Job had believed in goodness so hard that it amounted to badness. He had believed in himself as generous till stinginess had seemed criminal to him. He had not seen the highest truth, that there is no generosity to praise and no parsimony to hate in the Absolute. He had kept himself so strictly against bribery and deception that he hated bribery and deception. He had to make the one bold plunge past thinking that in the realm of the Divine there is either honesty or dishonesty. Unto whom should the One Mind be honest? Against whom could truth itself be dishonest?

From whom could all Power take power? These were the questions, which the failure of his belief in reward for goodness and punishments for wickedness urged upon him. Feeling them to be unanswerable from any plane of moral law, he was torn by the inherent nature of the questions out of the clutches of the moral law into the gospel of free grace. Between him and the miser there was in Divine Mind no difference. All that had been called difference was self-righteousness. It was recognizing differences in the One Undifferentiated Universal.

Slowly but surely, the sun of joy rose in the east of Job's mind with this humble acknowledgement. Health was restored. Friends returned to honor him as of yore. Flocks and herds were bestowed upon him. All these were the symbolic signals of the new mind into which he had come, wherein he saw clearly that there is no high or low, no rich or poor, no learned or unlearned, no good or bad in the mind of the Absolute.

The recognition of this truth was his touch of Power itself face to face. Without goodness or badness, without wisdom or foolishness, simply by touching Power itself, all the signs of power in joyous existence fell across his pathway.

The verses selected for this lesson are the words of Eliphaz the Temanite, while he is trying to convince Job that if he had been thoroughly good he would not have had calamities. There must be some secret vileness in his nature, or environments would not arrange themselves so vilely about him. He rehearses the conditions, which swing around the good and pious. He hints at the terrible things men and nature are guilty of, whose terrors are only to be avoided by acknowledging one's self, guilty of soil.

Job sees that he is, in some mysterious way, out of joint with divine order, but that is not by inherent vileness he is certain. *"Thou knowest that I am not wicked."* (Job 10:7) he cries in desperate fearlessness of a God frowning upon the least crime in His offspring. It took him many, many days to reason it out that it was his own belief in goodness as valuable over badness that hid him as a veil hides from the one only Power which recognizes no distinctions, but rains upon the harvest fields of all men alike, too pure to behold iniquity, and too free to be caught by the doctrine of goodness.

These eleven verses are descriptive of the delights, which come from sight of the free universal spirit. Eliphaz saw that blessed conditions are evidences of divine favor, but he had one flaw in his reasonings. There is no God to make sore and to bind up. The Absolute does nothing. Recognizing the Absolute does all. The less of the Absolute we recognize, the less is done.

This principle of recognizing or not recognizing, works on every plane. By a process of reasoning, every mind becomes receptive. In those receptive moments, whatever is recognized first, acts first. Put your mind to arguing for itself as being bound to keep inside certain lines end at some point along the way, it will be soft and humble to its own arguments. That moment fixes your destiny till you take to another argument for your-self from some premise more like the free Absolute. Put your mind to arguing from the idea of itself being under any law of necessity and find yourself from some moment of your life's pathway obliged to put up with conditions and make the best of situations thrust upon you.

When the mind is softened, as putty in the fingers of the glazier, to its own arguments, it is important what religious teachings or what sights or sounds touch it face to face. The children are set to certain life arguments. The pictures of an agonized Jesus hang in their homes. The pictures of men and women whose lives were troubled stare at them everywhere. At the softened moments they touch face to face the mind that has argued for hardship and suffering. Yet none of it is of the Divine Mind. Blessed is he who, taking an impregnable premise, argues without distraction to the softened mood of Job, and with eyes fixed on love itself, feels the touch of Power itself on his spirit, sees the free beauty of life itself as it paints the pathway of his own beautiful life as it has waited forever to recognize it.

Under one dispensation Job boasted that he had not meddled with things too high for him. Under the other dispensation, "Nor height nor depth nor any other creature could separate him" from the One in whom is no variableness nor shadow of turning from supreme greatness, from the One whom to know is life without death in its cup, strength without weakness to baffle, peace without hardship, health without sickness, beauty for ashes, prosperity without want.

This was the gospel of Jesus Christ to the world. None so poor, that he may not come up and eat of it, and prove it in a new unhindered life. With such an argument to soften the mind of man, how the heavenly city of God will dawn on his vision instead of earth's struggling scenes! This once fixed on his soul's plastic pages: *"Behold! I have set before you an open door which no man can shut"* (Rev. 3:8).

Job's argument put into language suited to each individual is the best argument on record for speed in softening and humbling the mind to its impressionable point. He took his own name from the day of his birth according to the belief of the world and denied that in or about him as a new-born child fresh from Divine Spirit were there any causes or results of causes that could lead to disgrace, poverty or failure. He prophesied for himself at every season of his life, as it appeared to be that the reality as it is according to untrammeled Health, Prosperity and Peace should be manifest in the eyes of his age. Thus he made solid foundations for his present life to stand upon, and strengthened and toned the quality of his mind to be able, at its meekest moment, to receive the richest blessings which recognition of the One Power here waiting has to bestow.

Inter-Ocean Newspaper, April 9, 1893

LESSON III

STRENGTH FROM CONFIDENCE

Book of Job, Part II

Thomas Carlyle said that neither in the Bible nor out of it is there anything written of equal literary merit with the Book of Job.

There has never yet been a good translation of it, and therefore many of its literary beauties are lost to the readers of the English version. Martin Luther tried faithfully to render into German the difficult Hebrew in which the book is written, and finally said, "I am sure Job is suffering more from my version than from the taunts of his friends."

There is no hint anywhere in the Book or out of it as to who wrote it. He is the "Great Unnamed." Dean Bradley tells us that the birthday of this most splendid flower of Hebrew poetry has been sought for up and down among the centuries and cannot be found. Many call it an epic poem because, like Homer's Odyssey and Virgil's Aeneid, it is the story of a hero, a long struggle, a conquest. It tells the story of a soul meeting face to face its own shadow and seeing how darkly human existence spreads its mysterious joys and sorrows before him. It explains the stately goings of the spiritual life in the soul from the midnight watch on Egypt's dark sands of failure and sorrow to the horizon line of a morning in Paradise.

Job tells how prosperity comes to them that set their minds to prosperity and how prosperity is also the fruits of righteousness. He shows that successes and triumphs which a man has won by force of will and determination are temporal, and reach their boundary line somewhere as poverty and defeat. He proves that honors, wealth, pleasure resulting from righteousness are also temporary, reaching their end the sooner the more godlike a man's goodness proves to be, that he may come into his possessions by that other premise which is beyond righteousness — which is by the Jesus Christ mind.

Last week, the argument of Eliphaz, who was still harping on the law of righteousness and its fruits, was given. Job knew the science of righteousness as well as his friends. He was surprised that they did not see that his case was past the application of doctrine and needed some inspirational treatment never yet practiced by any of them. When a man has acted up to the highest light he has had from the days of his youth up, and on through manhood, giving all that he had and knew to his ideals of right as instructed by his religion, and at the end thereof he is the most afflicted and despised creature in his community, the religion he has been practicing has touched the heights of its ministry upon him. He must spring past it into some higher light with healing in its beams potent enough to touch his case or his eyes will not view many daylights on earth. His belief in death will fold him round.

Job began at the beginning and rehearsed the science of righteousness. He gave the twelve points of the law exactly as we have them now. He showed how carefully he had kept them and how prospered he had been by so doing. He tells his friends that the instant he finds that point which is beyond righteousness he *"shall come forth as gold"* (Job 23:10); he sees plainly that there is a point. His friends think that it is blasphemy to see that there is a light brighter than righteousness. Job rises to the glorified speech of despair and calls for a God who is not as man.

Suddenly he found that hatred of evil is as much acknowledging the power of evil as doing it. He found that believing in righteousness and unrighteousness is ungodlike. He sees that if he would be the soul lighted by the face of its Maker, he must be too pure to behold iniquity. He must not be righteous to escape unrighteousness. In the deeps where he had been finding Hades, he must see only God. *"If I make my bed in hell, Thou art there"* (Psalms 139:8).

He found that there is a strength that comes from a strong belief in one thing or other, true or false, which reached its limit in one or the other generation. A belief in a man's mind that he fears the face of no man living may make him strong in his bodily frame for many years. But that strength will be temporal, however many generations it stays in his family mind. It is an idea which will strengthen a nation that holds it as it did Germany, whose Kaiser renewed the former proclamation. But it will meet defeat somewhere, for it has no foundation to stand on.

Job saw that strength may come from confidence in the presence and championship of a divine being, but that strength also is transient for it carries with it the idea of a weakness without the championship of that being. The strength that alone could infuse itself through his being must be out of the reach of the insidious poison of belief in a weakness to be saved from. It must be the strength of some being whose strength was not the opposite of weakness, but unchallenged might. *"Would He contend with me in the greatness of His power?"* (Job 23:6)

Job believed in the renewal of youth by physical practices, temporarily, and also in the renewal of youth by a process of right thinking. Elihu had a mind that could not communicate young vigor to those who received its treatment. His thoughts were invigorating and buoyant because they were about the spirit in man and its inspiration of almightiness (Job 32:8) — *"There is a spirit in man; and the inspiration of the Almighty giveth them understanding."* But Job was out of reach of Elihu's mind treatments because that young man had not demonstrated his own vital elixir by the action of that spirit which Job admitted was in him. *"Is not my help in me?"* (Job 6:13) said Job; of course it is; it has a law of its own for laying hold upon the universal elixir, which is the only thing that can save me, but it is not the fact of my spirit being one in kind and power with the spirit of God and I want to be told; you must show me how to use my spirit to lay hold on the Universal Spirit so as to be restored to the days of my former strength and prosperity in a security not threatenable with loss, or I might as well die now as later on. It is not your treatment I want in this day of my calamity, but the inspiration of your practical experience of laying hold on something, which drew you out of a situation equal to mine and set your feet safe on an eternal rock.

His friends could not understand such a state of mind. They felt that if there was a possibility of curing inflamatory pains by their spiritual enlightenment, whether they had experienced the same or not, that must be the way of curing all things. They felt that if putting away a secret fault would cure palsy,   putting away a secret fault must also cure boils.

They thought that Job's talk argued that he was righteous in his own eyes.

That was not true. Job's righteousness was what he believed to be the righteousness of the God in him at its highest power of demonstration on the earth. He had honestly believed that it would keep any man well and prosperous all his days. He saw now that it was not so; that the highest righteousness taught by religion would not save a man from calamity and sickness any more than the straightest wickedness. He now understood that advice in Ecclesiastes 7:16, which reads *"Be not righteous overmuch . . . Why shouldest thou destroy thyself?"* It was a terrible disappointment to him, but out of it all he came forth with the knowledge of how to lay hold upon the unresponsible Absolute for life, health, strength, support and defense, which have no opposites.

The whole Book of Job represents the whole book of every man's mind. If any man will study that book and understand the mysterious connection between Job and God, he will discover his own true relation to the same Being and come into the possession of all the blessings of the universe by a way, which is not the accident of opportunity or the fruitfulness of goodness.

Satan stands for the mind's fear of evil. Notice that Job said he had never been free from the fear of coming to want, old age, misery (Job 3:25-26). The Lord is the law that operates with thoughts whereby "thought in the mind has made us what we are"; it is the regulation of cause and effect. God is that certainty, far away in the regions of mind, that there is something absolute. The certainty itself is the Absolute. Satan is the ruler over mind, apparently. Fear of coming to want makes men work. Fear of sickness makes them diet, and fear of accident makes them avoid places and occasions. Fear of being thought ignorant makes them study. Fear of their children going wrong makes them severe. Fear of being thought ill of makes them silent, makes them go to church, makes them dress uncomfortably. Fear of old age, fear of losses, fear of ostracism — all this is Satan.

The law of fear is a good law; it is the same as the law of right thoughts in that it comes out somewhere in the body, or the home, or the social life. If intellect fails, fear of something or other did it. If memory is gone, fear of something or other ate it up. If accidents or losses come, they plainly tell you what special fear "going to and fro over the earth" of your mind hurried to the surface just then.

This is the Lord allowing Satan to torment Job, because actual communication with the God region of mind would never make a man move to right or left through fear of losing reward or meriting punishment. "He who knows Me is Myself," is the God word, and he who is God does not earn life or health or strength or possessions. He who is God loses nothing, gains nothing.

Job settles the question of there being a continual pressure of the God in man to unite with the God without in demonstrating unhindered happiness by showing that it can be done. He lost fear of all kind and thus from walking under the reign of Satan he walked under the shadow of God. At the last he saw that righteousness is fear of punishment since sure victory over temptation is from the fear that temptation yielded to will spoil the soul. To God in man there is no temptation, nothing to resist, therefore no righteousness. Dwelling on this theme brought his mind up as by a strong rope into the presence of God.

He, who learns the lesson of Job as it is meant for him, need not fear for the fears of his lifetime to come to the surface in their peculiar calamities. He may take his Satan by the neck now and hurling him out of his mental universe walk forever free in the light of God.

Job mourned for a "daysman (a mediator) betwixt" him and his Absolute God. At first he said there was none. *"There is no daysman betwixt us that might lay his hand upon us both"* (Job 9:33).

Then he found that his own words were his daysman, for in their hottest fires of feeling they told such truth of the Absolute God that he admitted: *"Even now, behold, in heaven is my Witness, and mine Advocate is on high"* (Job 16:19).

So, on the battlefield of every man's mind, his fear that has ruled him having done its worst in calamity, he may turn away from his calamity and his fear and talk to the God in himself that knows no fear till he realizes that his own argument is his advocate with the Father. His own argument being utterly reasonable like Job's in his Jesus Christ.

"For we know that we have an advocate with the Father" (I John 2:1). Any time we please to use this high argument for the divinity within ourselves, and its omnipotence, we are having the active influence of the living Jesus Christ. *"Is not my help in me?"* (Job 6:13)

Many writers who admire the beauty of this great poem still insist that Job did not at all settle the question of how a man can be reconciled to the misfortune of the upright. There is a clear explanation, therefore, in the admission which he makes of his always having acted from fear. He even feared he might lose his fear of the Almighty. Genung, whose translation of Job is considered the best, says:

"Job's trembling solicitude lest he should lose hold of his fear of the Almighty passed away when he faced death, and in its place rose a boldness before God which mounted to the amazing height of his everlasting 'No' to the idea of his friends that God was punishing him. And as he neared the mercy seat, where all is love, his fear was so cast behind him that his whole being was melted. He knew he had not got to die to come into God."

"I from my flesh shall see God, whom I shall see for myself: whom mine eyes shall behold a stranger no more" (Job 19:26-27).

The fear, which stirs the upright man, is as much his Satan as Job's fear was Satan. High reasoning about the God within us who was never responsible for calamity or pain, who seeth not as man seeth, is a daysman betwixt us and our omnipotent, changeless God. With one touch on the Absolute God and one on our human life, our high reasoning with the Almighty bind us to love that casteth out fear.

The very demonstrations of Job are ours. What lack had he when his daysman had pleaded his cause? What sickness worse than his has ever been healed? What joys greater than his have ever enchanted the life of man? What more inspiring theme has man's warfare or loving ever been than Job's fight for his freedom from Satan, that all men might also be free?

Inter-Ocean Newspaper, April 16, 1893

LESSON IV

THE NEW DOCTRINE
BROUGHT OUT

Book of Job, Part III

There is a new theory about the duality of the brain. It has many believers. They are sure to be prepared by thinking of the brain in that way (explained by Dr. Richardson in the Asclepiad for December) for welcoming esoteric interpretations of the Bible.

By that theory each of us has a double brain. The two brains are seldom balanced in any of us. One of our brains may be half under water, leaving the other brain to do all the thinking. Then when the useful one has got badly worn and does not receive impressions well, a different way of thinking will plunge that one under water and raise the well-rested one to activity.

They account for the religious conversions of so-called dissolute people on this plane. Great excitement will plunge the responsible bad brain downward and raise the ready but hindered brain upward. Whatever causes the excitement will first impress the uncovered brain.

Granted that the brain exhibits these phenomena — that excitement will submerge the worn-out brain and that which causes the excitement will impress its character upon the sensitive fresh one — it is important that we take the best excitant if we would have the best thinking character. This up and down of material we notice is caused by ideas; so ideas are masters of the brain. There must be some ideas, which are true. Those ideas must be more exciting and powerful than false ideas. In religious excitement, the idea of a wrathful God and day of judgment has been very powerful in plunging old half brains downward and raising complementary ones upward. The consequence has been that we have had a world of strong advocates of the punishment theory and very slight expounders of the kindness theory.

This is the third and last lesson in Job. According to the dual brain teaching, poor Job had worn his first half brain nearly to death with talking and thinking about the law of that God who had thrust him into human existence foolish and naked, and punished him severely for every mistake he made trying to know and get clothed. In his old age, he harvested the crop of his lifelong fear lest he might come to want. It was mixed with his lifelong knowledge that he had done everything he knew to keep the wrathful and easily offended

Deity appeased. He had fulfilled the law of righteousness. He had lived in perpetual fear. These two religious teachings faithfully kept had run their full course in him. They ended in poverty, disgrace and pain. Then arose, the argument, which every mind uses, either feebly or strongly, for the rights due the sentient creatures thrust into human environments ignorant and naked. In the sublime excitement of reasoning from the loftiest conceivable standpoint, Job's worn-out brain fell out of weight, and the new thinking suddenly impressed the uplifted convolutions.

His last doctrine was the mighty teaching that the Divine Original from whence all alike sprang, having made us out of His own substance, we are in nothing whatsoever different from Him. If we seem to be different, it is because we have spread before ourselves a panorama of imaginations impressed upon our respective estates by wrong teachings. Job shows that persistent holding on to a reasonable promise will rouse itself to white heat some time and furnish excitement enough to bring up the fresh brain and charge it with impressions quite independent of former thoughts. Under the reign of the new doctrine, he was mightily blessed both within and without.

He demonstrated the proclamation of Jesus Christ that the kingdom of harmony or heaven would be on earth when the spiritual conceptions of bliss in the heart should be outwardly shown by good health, good judgment and prosperity.

It is noticeable how speedily his new doctrine wrought itself out for him, while the old ideas had taken years to bring his calamities to view. There is rising now all over the world a new kind of reasoning. It takes up the idea firstly that if we came forth from Spirit we must be spirit; if we came forth from Good we must be good. At this point Job cried with a loud voice: *"Thou knowest that I am not wicked for Thy hands fashioned me"*(Job 10:7-8).

As this cry arises now from the multitudes who have been told that they are sinners for so long that their old brain no longer cares whether they are or not, they lay hold upon the next exciting proposition, viz.: *"The Spirit of God is in my nostrils"* (Job 27:3). *"Till I die I will not remove mine integrity from me"* (Job 27:5). *"My heart shall not reproach me as long as I live"* (Job 27:6). *"I will maintain my cause"* (Kings 8:45; 2 Chron. 35:39). The pull upward of the strong mind, which this persistence makes, is wonderful. By it we learn that there is nothing so powerful as speaking from the spiritual standpoint.

Job was very hardy and vigorous in his denial of his being anything but spirit after he got started. Jesus Christ told all who heard Him preach to deny themselves vigorously. No man upon earth is our father. God is our Origin, He said. It is the character of truth to set free from bondage. If we are not free we must be speaking lies and not truth. Poverty, pain, grief, are bondage. Those who have them are taking the past teachings of worn-out religions. The ever new teaching of Jesus is: *"The truth shall make you free"* (John 8:32). *"God is Spirit"* (John 4:24). *"God is your Father"* (John 8:41).

This is speaking from the spiritual standpoint. It is rarefying already the atmosphere that envelopes the world. The old heaven impressed on the old brain fades from the mind. The old earth impressed upon the old cognitive plates falls on our vision. We can only see what we believe in. As by Job's steady description of the unfailing joyousness and wisdom which reasoning from the spiritual standpoint would give, he wrought out a new environment, so by the steady description of what rights are due the people of this planet shall the transcendent glory of heaven fold them all around.

"The inhabitants shall not say I am sick any more" (Isaiah 33:24).

Job had a fearful struggle with the consequences of his lifelong fear. He found that nothing whatsoever but the highest and strongest reasoning from the proposition of his being spirit would save him. As a spiritual being he knew he could make no mistakes. He ignored his flesh nature. This was the height of wisdom. Jesus told us that the flesh profiteth nothing. If we are in great calamity of any sort and feel that if we had done differently it would now be very well with us, we have to get very strongly excited on the proposition that the spirit never makes mistakes. If the spirit in us never made mistakes, then no mistakes were ever made. The talks about mistakes are "Job's comforters." Let us have none of them. *"God forbid that I should justify you,"* persisted Job to those who believed in mistakes. (Job — Chapter 13)

From the spiritual standpoint the world is now able to throw down all the things it has been taught and come up out of its drowned state into the freedom of spiritual light.

"As when by drastic lift of pent volcanic fires

The dripping form of a new island springs to meet the air,

So from my grief I rose."

The weight of fear falls into the sands of nowhere when the spiritual doctrine rises. *"The dragon is cast down"*(Rev. 12:9), prophesies John.

According to Aristotle, that is "the best condition of things which produces not the largest amount of knowledge or wealth, but the men of noblest nature." In Froude's inaugural address as professor of history at Oxford, he insists that we have not through all the ages of civilization made any distinct progress in productions of this kind. How could we when we have been taught that we are temporal, limited, sinful flesh? He goes on to deplore the distinctions between rich and poor and the irredeemable poverty and sadness of the masses. How could they be any different under the dominant teaching that there is a great Being sitting on a throne striking down the innocent victims of birth into ignorance through material differences?

Did Jesus Christ come prophesying of a world believing on His doctrine and crying with cold and hunger? There is now somewhere arising one who shall be a living demonstration, example, and teacher of how the truth of Jesus applied will be a practical gospel to the poor. They shall not look forward to heaven for protection and rest; they shall get it by the dip of their former ideas under the horizon waters of oblivion and the rise of their assimilation with the meanings of Jesus.

Some commentators have written that Job's prosperity straight from his new ideas was "a sad concession to a low view of providential dealings." They think that the author descended from the lofty pinnacle where imaginary beings float around in imaginary heavens oblivious of the rights of men to tell of how Job's outward prosperity on this plane agreed with his descriptions of divine kindness.

This divorce of the without from the within in the theology of the ages has divorced men from women, mind from peace, children from homes, religion from practice. It is not decent for Christ to wear the seamless robe, and own the bread, meat, milk and wine of all the worlds. It is not decent for Him to touch the leper and make him clean. It is not decent for Him to pay the taxes of His age. So Job rises in the scale of wisdom, and by his patience in holding on to his exciting argument touches the hem of the priceless robe of the Lord Jesus Christ.

"Ye have heard of the patience of Job, and have seen the end of the Lord, that the Lord is very pitiful and of tender mercy" (James 5:11). Ye have heard that prosperity is of the Lord. This is the wisdom of the ages in a word. It produces universal nobility of character.

Inter-Ocean Newspaper, April 23, 1893

LESSON V

Wisdom's Warning

Proverbs 1:20-23

In the religious teachings a certain class of pious minds have always personified abstract principles. Jesus Christ did not personify, he illustrated. *"The kingdom of heaven is like unto,"* he said. He did not call poverty by a god's name, nor the expression of man's conviction of the reality of good by the name "Michael." He was willing to illustrate his mighty meanings by parables, but he said that coming in his perfect manifestation, he should not use parables, *"I will see you again and your heart shall rejoice, I shall no more speak unto you in proverbs, but I shall show you plainly of the Father."* It is noticeable that the very most spiritually free of young students of religious science now use hardly a similitude. They never illustrate. A parable they never speak unto us. Thus they are giving the Jesus Christ principle its highest expression through them.

Personification Of Wisdom

This lesson personifies wisdom. She is spoken of as crying aloud in the streets. Job heard the voice of God in the whirlwind. There is no doubt but the sounds on the street have running through them a fine enchanting call. There is no doubt but that every sentient creature has a hearing faculty capable of distinguishing the call and understanding its import.

Commence at Proverbs 1, 20-23 and read what this fine enchanting voice does and what it means. Wisdom is not a woman. The finesse and mercifulness of wisdom made certain seekers after wisdom call it a woman. Solomon so speaks of wisdom. So also does John in Revelations 12. The same with good. The power and majesty of the good itself caused many to call it a man. So we have the name "God," when the knowledge of how the absolute good acts suddenly spread into Job's consciousness he said he heard God's voice. Moses also, when his own mind understood its irresistible power, said that God called himself the I Am, as if he were a man. Here, when one knows without a doubt what it is best to do, best to say, best to think, Solomon calls it an invisible woman speaking.

There is one religion now practiced in the East, which personifies everything. If a man undertakes a task and meets an obstacle or hindrance, he says that the god of obstacles has met him. He attends carefully to those rites and ceremonies, which cause that god to retire from his pathway. The god of poverty is called Bimbogami. When that god gets hold of a man he will not be driven away, coaxed away nor propitiated in any way.   He is the meanest god that gets after a man. There is the god of penuriousness and the god of good luck. The peculiarity of those who personify principles is that they never fail to attribute human foibles and frailties to them. Then, like the Greeks, they made images of them, and like the heathen, they worship the images. Solomon was no exception. He fell to worshiping images. He says that those who will not heed the counsels of the invisible woman shall have great calamity and she will laugh at them and mock them in unpitying fashion when they are in their deepest distress. The veriest child can see that if woman is so revengeful as that, she is a dangerous thing to be turned loose on poor humanity who can not tell her voice from the sound of the cart wheels, yet who are to be terribly punished if they do not hear it.

Wisdom Never Hurts

The veriest child will prefer to be told that if he does the best he can and speaks the best he can, he is acting and speaking wisely and the next speech and action will be still wiser, "Do the duty that lieth nearest thee; thy second duty shall already have become clearer." The moment the child is told that if he does not do the best he can he will be punished, his mind revolts, because no child believes in punishment. The child is quite right, for wisdom never hurts or strikes. The teaching of punishment punishes; it is not goodness that punishes.

A great preacher proposed that we take our young ones down through the slums, the saloons, the poverty-stricken homes of drunkenness and terrify them into being good by the sight of badness. Now, if that plan were sufficient, those brought up in the slums and saloons would be archangels. We cannot have too much instruction in wisdom.

The teaching of punishment brings up methods of punishment. Mind, is logical; it arranges a whipping for not listening to the counsels of good men who, when they were young, were terrified into choosing between two very plain propositions — life and death. It arranges old age and lameness for those who do not choose between the spirit and matter. The punishment theory always keeps the idea of "two" going in the mind, as good and evil, Jesus and Satan, God and Devil, wisdom and foolishness, riches and poverty, strength and feebleness.

The "Two" Theory

Solomon was strong in the "two" theory. Jesus erased the whole "two" theory. *"Do not think I am come to condemn you." "Forgive them."* He told how upright and glorious all children are by nature. He never asked their mothers to show them the consequences of not loving and listening to Him. This is wisdom itself. We can not make the world demonstrate wisdom by pointing out foolishness. We

44

can not express wisdom by talking or thinking of punishments for foolishness. Goodness is the only reality. Wisdom is really the only voice speaking. God is the only Being. There is no devil. The mind of God is the only mind. There is no foolishness. The spirit of God is the only nature. There is no refusing to love and listen.

When we do personify principles we see that they are omnipotent and. formless. Then we see that they are in us and. through us and we could not get rid of them if we wanted to.   Solomon expressed it in the twenty-third verse, *"Behold, I will pour out My spirit unto you, I will make known My words unto you."*

The "two" theory has been obliged, to insist that God suffers. This is wisdom, for if there is only God, then if there is any suffering it certainly must be God and God only that suffers. That theory makes us obliged to say that if there is any sinner it must be God, for there is only one God. Also, if there is any foolish one it must be God, for all the universe cries out that God is the only Being. If there is any strife it must be God fighting, for there is only one God. If there is any refusal of the Spirit it must be God refusing Himself, for God is Spirit and absent from nowhere. Those who have whirled themselves around this necessity have seen that one mind in them and through them everywhere is saying: "I am satisfied with myself. I am the High and Holy One that Inhabiteth eternity. I am Wisdom. I am Strength. I am All. I am One."

Think over this reasoning and see how uplifted you will feel. Mourn over the scornful, the foolish, the hard-hearted, and see how depressed you will feel. Then watch the effect of your presence on people under the pressure of the different meditations.

As Solomon spent quite as much time in this lesson telling of the fools and simple and scornful as telling of the pourings out of the mighty Spirit and the everlasting speech of wisdom which no man can get away from, we do not wonder that there was such a divided condition claimed by his mind and that most of the good behavior of the world is veneering. The divided estate is no estate, and veneering is unreality. Let us tell the truth about God. The only Being we can speak of as God. With this key in your hand read the Proverbs. With this key read all Scripture. You will find a new world open to you.

The nearer you dwell to your knowledge of that principle that moves through you unrestrained, unchanged through the ages, the oftener you will speak words which will cause health to show forth. You will find every force in the world operating to make you express wisdom, life, beauty, strength. There is no plane of human experience upon which you can be living now that each item of it will not point your next step. In the conspiracy of Brutus against Caesar Shakespeare describes how full nature herself was of directions, even a stranger being made to thrust a scroll of written words into his hands telling him to stay at home.

In the conspiracy of the belief of two opposing elements in our human nature, the fine loving knowledge of the watch-care of the good calls out to us to fear nothing, to trust in the good, to walk out of the conspiracy by knowing there is no reality in it, no power in it, by hearing the voice that speaks at our own gate, and being satisfied. Not one in the pangs of sickness but hears his healing directions speaking so that even if he lives on the lowest plane of belief in nature he can understand them. In Russia they cause a live eel to swim itself to death in watke (a kind of white whiskey) and take the liquid to cure drunkenness. The Russian will assure you solemnly it has never failed to cure. In America the homoeopathist will plunge live honey bees in alcohol and use the liquid for erysipelas (acute infection of the skin). The faithful homoeopathists firmly believe in it. So the healing spirit "cries at the entering in of all the gates."

All is Spirit

To those who believe that all is spirit, and matter has no healing power in it, these are words full of fire and healing meanings given, and sometimes white waves of joyous elixirs, as feeling that the one Spirit moves on unhindered in beautiful health. Their Gateway is spiritual "feelings". Thus the wisdom of every mind is truly saying: "I will make known My words unto you." There is no situation into which we can come that this wise mind is not uttering directions into happy freedom. If one is burdened with tasks it seems out of his power to carry out, there, at his own gates, in his own language, in every movement of nature, and in every transaction, is information for freedom. This is Jesus Christ's gospel to the heavy laden. If one is in debt and can not be free let him hear the wind that moves through every circumstance telling him what Jesus Christ means by carrying on His own shoulders the cross of the world. For this wisdom that speaks always and forever of help and freedom and prosperity is the Jesus Christ wisdom. It never says, "If you do not do my way you will be punished", but forever, "This is your way to Joy; come!"

Whoever says that the goodness of wisdom warns of dangers or evil looks at the divine messages through Solomon's gates, not through the truth of the Christ who says, "I will give you rest, fear not." In the second coming of Christ to our gates we are not led by the language we now employ, with its references to freedom from pain, help from hardships, peace from turmoil. We shall be led to other gates where these were never named. There is a language suited to those who have risen, away from even the memory of their earthly experiences. The same wisdom speaks it that speaks to our present estate. There is but one wisdom.

When we have disputes and contentions we always find it is because they who wrangle are not hearing the voice of direction at their neighbor's gates, but only at their own gates, and yet their neighbors are as wise as themselves by the same teacher. There beyond contention, is only one language. There is One Lord and His name One. Whatever we are doing or thinking we are hearing wisdom at the gates of our present language. But on through the eternities that mind in us is able to lead, with messages ever suited to our eternal living. Today it tells loudly and clearly on the ear of the Christian that Christ brought a gospel to the poor that should take them into the providing Jehovah's gates; that He brought a gospel to the sick which is sure healing; that He brought a gospel to sin which is sure holiness. It is that there is only God and if there is any poverty stricken it must be that one. If there is any sick it must be that one. If there is any sinner, simple or foolish, it must be the only one. Thus every mind shall know itself to be the only mind and knowing this the prophecy of Jeremiah for this hour is fulfilled:

"Thy words were found and I did eat them, and Thy word was unto me the Joy and rejoicing of my heart; for I am called by Thy Name, O Lord God of Hosts."

Inter-Ocean Newspaper, April 30, 1893

49

LESSON VI

THE LAW OF
UNDERSTANDING

Proverbs 3

After the return of Berkeley, Bishop of Cloyne, Ireland, from a journey in France, he was stricken down with fever. On his recovery, Dr. Arbuthnot wrote in satiric vein to Dean Swift: "Poor Philosopher Berkeley has now the idea of health, which was very hard to produce in him, for he had the idea of a strange fever upon him so strong that it was very hard to destroy it by introducing the contrary one."

Evans, the metaphysician, said that it takes three years for a mind to change its fixed ideas or settled beliefs. Emerson wrote, "All that you call the world is the shadow of that substance which you are, the perpetual creation of the powers of thought, of those that are dependent and those that are independent of your will." If any of us have believed that the real world is as we had been thinking it was while we had the faculty for experiencing pain or sadness, it would, according to Evans, probably take three years for us to really believe that our world, as we had experienced it, was all a mirage, the shadow of our thought substance. But why do we need to believe it takes so long for us to believe what is true?

Shadows of Ideas

Berkeley had been working out the problem of his life and mind as related to his world. Finally he rejected the idea of abstract matter, concluding that all material things are shadows of our ideas, conscious and unconscious. Yet his mind never so practically realized what it was reasoning about that it threw out as a shadow of its reasoning a good sound body. It never got so powerfully hold of the lines of connection between thoughts and conditions outside that he could keep himself always alive.

The following (19th) century did not produce anyone who could keep the lines on his bodily conditions straight enough to prevent entering into old age or sickness of some kind eventually, though there were a number who held off a long time and had great power in keeping others from death, pain and insanity. There was quite a step gained in this century in the way of practical relation between theory and practice. But there seems still to be a good deal of faltering by the way.

It is still not uncommon for doctors and clergymen to write or speak to each other of metaphysicians in very much the same strain as Arbuthnot wrote of Berkeley. Emerson never managed the convolutions of his brain by his theories of the insubstantiality of matter up to the point of keeping them healthily supplied with gray matter, and passed on without well proving his propositions.   So also Evans, though he gave himself up to his metaphysical doctrines more entirely than Emerson.   If no one actually gives himself entirely to his doctrines, how can he entirely practicalize them?

Whoever wrote the third chapter of Proverbs, which is today's lesson, was a metaphysician. He gives to all metaphysical reasoners some definite, very helpful information. He speaks of the denials and affirmations which the logic of mental science calls for and tells their practical outcome. He speaks of the effect on the world in which we live of the touch on the mind of the sixth idea of Christian metaphysics. He tells all the last six points and their practical manifestations. Sometimes the sixth lesson has seemed almost too idealistic to execute any prosaic mission, but this writer, whether he was Solomon or Hezekiah, sings over the wastes of departed ages, a reassuring refrain. He tells us that it is a working principle.

The Sixth Proposition

The sixth proposition of the Science of Christ is this: that if you understand the meaning of a principle so that it is your illumination, the light by which you judge of events, you do not need to take active measures to carry out your understanding, for the law is that your understanding has an independent way of working out your life conditions. By this lesson we would see that one need not go into battle to fight a horde of enemies; his spiritual convictions would attend to his defenses without bayonets or powder. By it, we see that we need not take material remedies for our seemingly failing health, for the wisdom that moves independently through us by our recognition of certain principles will pick us up and put us into situations alive with health and strength for us. By it, we see that we do not need to go to law to protect our name or property, for the sight we have of the spiritual independence of defense by external efforts will turn every attempted attack upon us into transfiguring glory for us after its own methods.

This law of understanding is called "Lord" in this lesson. It affirms that the earth and the heavens around us will appear to us as they are in reality when we steadily keep on recognizing the Facts of the world. So far, we have had flashes of sight of the Fact that the earth, the sky, the business of life, are all entirely different from the way they seem. These flashes of realization have brought us many blessings. This writer of our lesson adds another thing which we say little about. He says we are able to keep these illuminated moments and make them as years. These moments are fraught with mighty demonstrations. One metaphysician suddenly found herself encircled by a beautiful light in a deeply dark night the instant after she had said, "The darkness shall be light, for God is the light of the darkness. I need no other light." A realizing sense of the mighty truth she was telling threw its own light around her and she plainly saw her way. There is the prophecy that when a great company of men and women understand that their spiritual understanding is God, the city where they dwell shall have no need of the light of the sun, nor of the moon.

What Wisdom Promises

Commencing at the 13th verse, note what Science, called Wisdom in the feminine (the woman of Revelation 12), here promises all who hold their realizations steady. The 11th verse explains what seems to be afflictions. They are the external- izetions of mixed theories. Berkeley had a theory that sickness was the out-showing of an idea, yet he kept on holding the idea which made sickness, for he had never had any knowledge of which idea it was that made it. He had, nevertheless, light or realization enough to make himself heard and felt, not only in his own; country, but in ours. He was also made strong and intrepid in many ways by his flashes of understanding. This writer assures us that we cannot see the whole blessedness of the executive power of our own illuminations except we keep them steadily. He makes us responsible for holding on to our realizations. Whoever enters the path of that reasoning which declares "All good is God," and "That which is not good is not God," has begun to work for himself in the most satisfactory way there is to work. *"The merchandise of it is better than the merchandise of silver, and the gain thereof than fine gold"* (verse 14).

Why is not this supremely true if at the flash of one moment's consciousness of it your supplies come in full measure without your struggling?

Our writer experienced the bounty of his spiritual consciousness at the very beginning of his investigations. He saw that he had what would make fine gold and therefore he need not be digging for gold. He had the substance; he did not care for the symbol. His light on his words threw them on the screen of his world as whatever he pleased in the line of his valuables.

A candle flame striking on a chair throws the shadow thereof on the wall. Throw the candle flame on a hat tree and it will make another shadow. Suddenly the light on these doctrines may strike on your health and show on the bodily wall a robust vision of bodily health. Sudden light on certain of these ideas will be symbolized in a good memory or a new lease of life. In our day, we have not had a single one who could move the candle and make exactly the images on his walls he wanted to make. Some who have light on these metaphysical doctrines get everything for themselves while they are trying very hard to throw the light on their neighbor's condition. These are wondering why they can heal and advantage themselves but cannot reach others.

Clutch on Material Things

Some who have worked for years on the metaphysical propositions in hope of becoming utterly healthy have got everything else pretty nearly except health. Others who would like their illuminated moments to give them the wherewithal to pay their taxes as easily as Jesus paid his and feed their families as easily as Jesus fed multitudes, have splendid health, but cling to their material business tightly because they cannot move their candles at their will to bring them the symbols of bounty.

Notice that the bounties of spiritual illumination are here associated with acceptance of the very first lesson. Notice that "long life" is made the fruit of denials. "Riches and honor" are the fruits of affirmation. The bountiful supplies of human existence are the external signs of illuminations on the first and third propositions of Science. The name here given to Science is Wisdom. John says of her in Revelation that she is clothed with the sun and has 12 stars. That is, the whole science of mind is enlightening. Each lesson shows its own illumination when it is accepted. No metaphysician of today has said that if you are poor and in lowly position you had better master, the first and the third lessons of the Science, but this ancient writer makes bold to say so.

"Length of days is in her right hand; and in her left hand riches and honor" (verse 16). "Left hand" is affirmation. Learn to affirm well if you are in

want. "Right hand" is denial. Learn to deny well if you are cut off in everything you undertake. "Length of days" may apply to endurance of anything. The second lesson is denial. *"Deny thyself,"* said Jesus Christ. It is used in systematic thought on the same day with the eighth lesson, which is all about endurance or continuance.

No metaphysician as yet has demonstrated over the inherent idea he has in his bones that if he gives himself entirely to spiritual doctrine he will have a rough time of it. Every prominent metaphysician has been roasted alive and sawn asunder by modern methods, as the out-showing of his clutch on the doctrine of suffering. This author of Proverbs 3 insists that no spiritually minded man or woman has a right to suffer the first iota. If they do, they have not laid hold in reality on either one of the lessons, for he teaches that while some lessons may bring one thing and some another in the way of new environments, either one of them is sure to keep the metaphysician from persecutions and causes of weeping. *"Her ways are ways of pleasantness and all her paths are peace"*(verse 17). So if we have any occasion to mourn or feel like mourning, we must begin at the beginning of our science as if we had never heard of it and work it out mentally over again.

The Tree of Life

The first lesson is also called the first taste of the "tree of life." Here (verse 18), tasting of the tree of life is made the first condition of happiness.

Continuation in tasting is everlasting happiness. For one cannot eat too much wisdom. One cannot have too much Science. Spiritual Science is a substance of which the more you eat, the freer you are — quite unlike eating of bread or cakes or potatoes.

The tree of life is Science. The story of Adam and Eve fallen into suffering and hardship because of having eaten of Wisdom is a fable. There was never any serpent. There was never any nakedness of which the Spirit was ashamed. There was no man except the thought of God. It is true that mind knows what would be the opposite of itself. But that knowledge does not make the opposite of Spirit a genuine substance. If the Son of God is the thought of God, there is no making him anybody or anything else.

When the thought knows for an instant as a conscious cognition what is the opposite of good, it passes on instantly to knowing that the opposite is not existing. It knows the opposite as its own mental knowledge of what is not. There is all the story there is to tell of evil. Mind knows that the opposite of now is time. So all continuation or history of things that are not Spirit is a mental knowledge of what would be opposite to now if now were not all. But now is all and now is Spirit, the only substance; love the only law; good the only origin. This is the first idea which the high metaphysics of today bases its following ideas upon. This author proclaims that the life begins afresh with seeing that this is the first truth to state.

John tells us that this doctrine is a river of the water of life flowing from the throne of God and the Lamb. God is the good from which all things come that are come. The Lamb is the sun or thought which thinks of good as the only principle. He tells us that the tree of life bears 12 manner of fruits. We all know that the 12 lessons have each their particular and peculiar effects. This section of Proverbs asserts what these lessons do, especially the first three and the sixth. The rest of them, the author says, we must first get from out the secret of retaining our realizations. Thus it takes the eight lessons pursued thoroughly to learn how to hold the illuminated moments long enough to set the candle thereof around upon our life experiences just where we want them to shine out.

Prolonging Illuminated Moments

This third chapter of Proverbs tells of intelligence and of renewal of youth as results not obtained till we have learned how to prolong our illuminated moments. The metaphysician who saw the light of her words shining like a lamp did not keep the realization except for a little while. Another metaphysician was, by some peculiar denials he made, lifted out of the reach of everything material for one full week, during which time he healed deformities, chronic diseases, tumor, and every other supposition by the simplest words his mind put out toward them. Then he suddenly stopped. He had not got the first fruit of the eight lessons. This fruit, being continuance in sight of the action of Spirit through the mind, will lead up to all the other fruits of understanding. This metaphysician's miraculous powers at healing all manner of disease lasted while his hold on his illumination endured.

Our chapter speaks a great deal of the "walk," the "path," the "feet." It is not yet time to put forth the entire meaning given by Proverbs to the "feet." Out of the great significance of the feet as symbols of understanding, the symbolic acts of the washing of the feet and the kissing of the feet began. It takes the highest spiritual illumination to treat the feet successfully.

John fell at the feet of the angel because he who is meek and lowly of heart instinctively creeps close to that symbolic part of the being which represents the highest, the strongest, the surest understanding. When a metaphysician sees his patient's malady dropping toward the feet, he knows it will be gone entirely when he sees him again. This result of treatment is symbolic of the flowing downward from the over-bending and ever-descending wisdom from on high. Because the feet have been called the inferior symbols, much has been missed. People have supposed the head to be the special symbol of the understanding. This is only supposition. He that hath ears to hear let him hear angels and archangels singing, "At Thy feet we meekly kneel!"

Woman is the symbol of the Holy Ghost or motherhood of God. She has always been kept under, placed in lower positions by belief in sex differences. Thus the Holy Ghost ministry has been ignored. *"The Holy Ghost shall teach you all things"* (Luke 12:12), promised Jesus. The feet symbolize the teaching power of the Godhead. They represent the understanding of Spirit — the Holy Ghost of God. God hath chosen that the unknown, the ignored, the hidden, the foolish things of this earth shall confound the mighty and prudent in the last days of belief in distinctions, partialities, differences. How startled mankind will be to find that their feet are charged like electric clouds with intelligence concerning things kept secret from the foundations. *"For now hath He put down the mighty from their seats and exalted them of low degree."*

Inter-Ocean Newspaper, May 7, 1893

LESSON VII

SELF-ESTEEM

Proverbs 12:1-15

Take note of the multitude of people mourning
and discouraged over accusations which they have
allowed to cross their mental frontiers. We have it
recorded of two illustrious men that they understood how to close their mental gates on all the
thoughts they chose to exclude. They practiced this
so persistently that one reported he could fall
asleep any moment and not an idea would dare to
disturb him. The other could dictate letters on
widely different plans to six or eight people simul-
taneously.

What not to think and when not to think it is a
fine art. It is as wonderful a feat to master as what
to think and when to think it. In mental science
the second lesson is devoted to what not to think
and how to close the frontiers of our splendid mental country so as not to admit accusations. Its
sublime promise is that such refusals make us
strong and self-poised. They give the rest of the

thoughts freedom to increase and enlarge. We are certain by this process to think richly and truthfully about who we are by nature, where we came from, and what we are about. We find that we do not by our actual nature need reproofs. It was by letting reproofs get through our frontiers and being cast down thereby that we afterward seemed to deserve them. This is true of every man, woman and child, without exception.

Solomon on Self-Esteem

Our lesson today is Proverbs 12:1-15. Solomon here speaks to those who were calloused by opinions of themselves which they received into their mental precincts when they were young. *"He that hateth reproof is brutish"* (verse 1). The old earl, in the story of Little Lord Fauntleroy, was softened by the boy's direct address to his goodness, not by the reproofs of his relatives. This direct address to a man's God-born goodness can be made mentally. The old earl was melted by his daughter-in-law's persistent mental praises of him; not by his tenants' mental curses. There is not a man so seemingly hard or hateful but can be brought out from the rough by the skillfully put praise of his God-inherited temper. The jasper stone, clear as crystal, lies at his foundations. Calling him not brutish or wicked is the lapidary stroke that exposes him as he is.

So out from our own mind it is well that we put Solomon's descriptions of the two kinds of men. There are not two kinds of men. There is only one kind. *"Judge not according to appearances."* *"Whoso loveth instruction loveth knowledge"* (verse 1), says the proverb. The eager willingness of every creature to hear the truth about heaven and earth and itself from the moment it can ask questions is evidence that from the beginning, the spirit of man tendeth to knowledge. By one bold strike of the hammer of the doctrine of this hour, we break down the accusation that there is one who did not love knowledge when he came into our midst fresh from his Maker's wisdom.

"A good man obtaineth favor of the Lord: but a man of wicked devices will he condemn," reads the 2nd verse. It reads as if there were a formulated being on some high seat condemning and justifying mankind according to the accident of their bringing up. Did such a being exist it would be utterly impossible to love him. But there is not such a being. All actions and speech are the results of agreeing or not agreeing with accusations. Their logical outcome is the Lord. Their procedure is the law. This principle is God. No matter what idea or premise a mind takes, the idea has attraction in it sufficient to draw everything like itself to itself. Let a man think luck is against him intensely and it will act like a magnet to draw every condition of unhappiness he has given it energy to draw. Nobody sent him his misfortunes. Nobody favors or condemns him as a Supreme Judge might favor or condemn by bringing upon him what he calls misfortunes.

The Magnetism of Passing Events

As steel filings hurry to cling to a magnetic bar, so hurry events to their proper sentiments. Man charges any idea he pleases with his strongest emotion. The melted ointment hurries to fill the alabaster boxes. Hot emotions run for expression. Events come trooping to verify the value of expression. If the results are unloved it is no fault of Supreme God, nor in any sense offensive to Him. The principle was in the beginning, is now, and ever shall be the same that man stands master of destiny. He can turn the most intense idea, loaded with intensest anger, out of his borders any instant and give to whatever words from the Scriptures he pleases the sanction of his passion of love or hate or anger, or indignation, compassion, or fear. This will make him great. It will give him the free, wide feeling that nothing can interfere with him.

Take the raging emotions of your mind, turn them into some majestic mold. Shall a man say, "How terrible my lot is! I must steal for a living"? Nehemiah praised the Lord of Hosts while he was in deepest anguish. So his work progressed as if a mighty host wrought with him. No man needs to say, "I have to do it," when he employs little children or slays innocent animals. He need not make his idea of necessity his magnetic one. He need not live under a law of necessity whose results he condemns so hard that he finally verily thinks some great God is condemning him.

Nothing Established by Wickedness

The next part of our proverb (verse 3), reads that the root of the righteous is never moved, while nothing is established by wickedness. There does come a time when men perceive that the ideas their forefathers put so much vehemence into brought forth sickness, poverty, crying. Even "great" religious precepts shake and fall. Take that one which made for anarchy, namely, that even if we should pray and fast and give alms continually, God would never be satisfied that we had done enough. It falls, while the great kindly sentence that God saw all the work of His hands to be very good comes smiling into favor. Events which we do not like hurry forward and fall away faster because we put them into the hothouse of stronger expressions than we gave to our great principles. Nehemiah's temple, once built on the attractive strength of his magnifying the Lord, was an enduring monument, while Sanballat's eagerly pursued devices had their short successes and disappeared.

There was a certain Christian woman who fell prostrated with grief when she heard that she and her children were almost paupers. Closing her bedroom door she prayed three days and three nights that God would fulfill His promises to the widow and the fatherless. Her lot seemed utterly unfair. Suddenly, she gave all her despair into the enduring truth that there is bounty and support for every creature.

So great is this sentence that it requires great vigor of some kind to fill it. Then came such an assurance of assistance that a great joy seized her. She laughed with delight. This is the promise which she fulfilled: "At destruction and famine thou shalt laugh." The help came instantly. It was plenty and it lasted. Had she wailed out some other expressions she would have drawn other results.

Strength of a Vitalized Mind

She then began to fulfill another promise put into these proverbs, *"The mouth of the upright shall deliver"*(verse 6). She was a powerful helper of other people. Her mental energy was put into a reviving principle. It put out everything contrary to it. All her words fruited in satisfaction exactly as promised in the 14th verse of our lesson. Thus can one vitalize his mind to healing and put away from his premises all manner of disease. His neighbors who have thrown their energies into ideas which draw sickness -will feel his vivifying faith changing those ideas. They will be cured.

The 8th verse tells us: *"A man shall be commended according to his wisdom."* The commendation must begin within himself. He magnifies what sentences he pleases. Nothing interferes with any man's judgments. He magnifies the sentences that enlarge brains, and his brains are not questioned as to their size. He magnifies the ideas that make great musicians, and he is acknowledged to be such because he has

68

fed with attentions the sentences that make musicians. One does not have to say, "I am a great musician"; he has to find out the sentences that he most believes in concerning music, and feeling their truth commends them highly. He does not naturally love to be interfered with; he must let his love of not being interfered with enlarge itself. It will naturally protect his profoundly sincere ideas concerning music, so his whole territory will be given to harmony; and because he commends it, the world will commend it.

Concerning the "Perverse Heart"

The next line (verse 8), about the "perverse heart" *"He that is of a perverse heart shall be despised."* means the same. The so-called "perverse man" worked with an idea he felt in himself was wrong because he received it as wrong. It took up all his energy. The rest of the world agreed with his greatness of "perversity." Both men were equally gifted with so much riches of mental opportunity. The question is: "Can a man unload one sentence of the energy he gave it and throw his force into another?"

Energy is eternal substance. It is subject to man's will. He may remove it from one manner of thinking to another. It is never too late to do so. The removal of the force of mind from one sentence to another is the removal of health, strength, vitality. Especially you will see this to be so when you withdraw from an interest in material things and set your interests to flowing through spiritual themes. You will renew at once. *"The just shall come out of trouble"* (verse 13); *"A man shall be satisfied with good by the fruit of his mouth"* (verse 14). The opposites in this pair of proverbs show to the scientific mind only one thing, and that is the use of the universal energy equally distributed to and through each and every man for the enlargement of different sentences. There is no condemnation for any of them. There is no being anywhere waiting to condemn them. There is only principle. As we perceive this principle of energizing ideas till they cannot be penetrated by others, and cannot be interfered with, we see how impartial the Universal Mind is in giving to all alike the same unlimited supply of itself.

Inter-Ocean Newspaper, May 14, 1893

LESSON VIII

PHYSICAL VS. SPIRITUAL POWER

Proverbs 23:29-35

Law of Life to Elevate the Good and Banish the Bad *"First, the blade, then the ear, after that the full corn in the ear."*

This is the logic of events. This is science. The blade may be interfered with and never make the corn ear, but whatever takes the place of the corn has its blading time and full corn time. Some things blade and full so suddenly that their steps of change are not visible to the naked eye. This was the case of the loaves of bread manufactured by Jesus. This was the case with the thief on the cross. Jesus understood making one set of events absolutely invisible and putting another set in its place instantly. He did it by understanding spiritual government.

If we imagine obstacles where none exist and keep up the habit, we shall fill up the free highway

71

whereon we are walking with the manufactured limitations of imagination clear up to the blindness of eyes. Almost all middle-aged people, so called, have poor eyesight in consequence of unfounded apprehensions. If we keep listening to stories of material transactions, our ears will "wax gross" in some generation. Stories of spiritual courses never stop in the head, they are free and cannot be stored like the stories of inert matter. When a spiritual story is told, the material story must get away out of sight and hearing at once. Matter is liquid, and ether, and disappearance, to spirit.

"The earth is clean dissolved before me" (Isaiah 24:19). A very little spiritual feeling will make a very great change to matter when it comes against it. A grain of it will move a mountain out of the way. Peloubet tells us that if we put heaven and Christ and salvation to withstand the appetite of drink, it has such government over a man that he will trample them all under feet to gratify it. This is giving great power to physical mountains and no power to heaven and Christ. The spirit must seem a very feeble element of the universe to one who can say this. And so it must have seemed to the writer of Proverbs 23:29-35, which is today's Bible lesson.

Lesson Against Intemperance

It is called a lesson against intemperance. It discusses it entirely from the standpoint of matter. The writer expects to make intemperance disappear from its seeming enormity into nothingness by describing its blade and ear and full corn of process in getting the mastery of men. Generations of men before him had tried the same process and seen intemperance fatten on their descriptions. Generations since his time have practiced describing the omnipotent power of alcohol and they also have seen intemperance thrive on their fodder of description.

All intemperance asks to grow and enlarge upon its description of itself over and over as a terrible, enormous, strong, captivating force. If a whole body of men and women keep faithfully at it talking of its history from first moving itself in enchanting sweetness down the young man's throat (verse 31), to the time when *"at last it biteth like a serpent, and stingeth like an adder"* (verse 32), they will see it performing that way over and over in greater and greater numbers of cases. If they are very projective and forcible with their descriptions it will take very strong-minded young men indeed to withstand the wind of their mental suggestions. Wine and beer and brandy will subtly convince them of their irresistible charms.

The Koran tells us that "there is a devil in every berry of grape." Who made the grape? Who put the devil into it? Who made all things? Who made the power of the word?

All that the omnipotent good in the universe asks to grow and strengthen upon is description of its greatness, its powerfulness, its majesty and irresistible fascinations. Do you know of a whole body of men and women alive with joyous earnestness describing the mightiness and majesty of the spirit in man as it rises and marches over the wrongs and evils of earth and puts them down and out in the darkness of oblivion, stronger and abler and more terrible in its splendor than all wrong and all evil together?

Good Must Increase

Any lesson against intemperance must not work to increase intemperance, innocently or guiltily, as this writer does in what Professor Phelps calls "the drunkard's looking glass." Hear how great government matter is credited with getting: "Who hath woe? Who hath sorrow? Who hath wounds without cause? *They that tarry long at the wine; they that go to seek mixed wine"* (verses 29, 30).

Wine is very happy to be described as thus powerful. All things imitate the joy of Spirit when it is being proclaimed as omnipotent. A well-told story of how the Spirit *"moveth itself aright"* (verse 31) from the first little blade of right doctrine about it, to the triumphant shouts of the full power thereof will be the lesson against intemperance which the right teacher shall teach. When you tell him that "wine is a mocker and strong drink is raging," he will say, "In the name of the Omnipotent Good, I deny it." He has just as good right to see his story fulfill itself in the destiny of mankind as you have. It is all a matter of what you believe within you, and it is a matter of what he believes within him. Whose belief is the more like Jesus Christ's, do you think?

Mankind goes about describing things as of great value which have no value. They make it out that gold is valuable. So gold feels very happy and rolls itself together in great piles for those who fight for it best and are willing to sell and give everything away in order to have it. Everything imitates the happiness of the Spirit at being called the greatest value, and the gathering together of gold is imitation of the greater and greater glory of the Spirit which fills and thrills mankind when they are willing to give and sell everything they possess for the Spirit.

Do you know anybody who has given all his possessions, all his time, all his energies, all his chances for human happiness, to find the Spirit that is so powerful that to know it is life and joy enough for a whole world?

To Know Goodness Is Life

When you do see such a one you "will never hear him describing the power of matter or re-hearsing how a glass of wine has self-increasing dreadfulness from captivating daintiness to the drunkard's grave. He will remember that practice makes perfect and will utterly ignore the practice of making alcohol move toward his vision as a power when it has no power. His science will be the Science of Spirit. He will reason of its presence and its mightiness till he woos it out from its invisibility into being manifestly the only God in heaven and in earth. God is Spirit. Nobody inclines toward intemperance. Without the metaphysical hurricane of influence toward alcohol made by those who want to win away from alcohol, nobody would ever get intoxicated. How do you suppose the metaphysical practitioners heal their patients of grievous swellings? They tell the story of the Spirit in man, its presence around man. Its goodness and health unalterable are praised over and over till it comes forth in its beauty from its hiding place under the swelling formulated by somebody's description of something bad that he had seen or heard. The bad story cannot resist the good story. The wind of the good gets to blowing as the heart of the thinker gets warmer, and away blow the gathered particles stored up as a bunch or burden of pain. This is the way to blow the highly piled mountain of alcoholic intemperance away off the planet.

Instead of describing the beginning of government as a glass of wine or brandy, let the heart and lips take up the song of the real moving of the beautiful Spirit that keepeth company forever with the sons and daughters of God. Instead of telling that *"thine eyes shall behold strange women and thine heart shall utter perverse things,"* sing in the secret music halls of the soul your glad promise that *"thine eyes shall see the King in his beauty"* (Isaiah 33:17), *and "thine heart shall rejoice in the God of salvation."*

The Angel of God's Presence

There has been very little said through the ages of the angel of God's presence that keeps company with every child through all its pilgrimage on earth, but there has been a great deal said about a Satan, a devil, an appetite, or tempter, or passion, accompanying everyone. He that would converse with his angel must not spend his breath talking of its shadow.

Unto Moses the great Principle of Good spoke as a voice saying, *"Behold! mine angels shall go before thee"* (Exodus 32:34). Jesus spoke of the angel that accompanies each child. (Matthew 18:10) He said nothing of any other influence because He knew that things grow on recognition. Isaiah said that an angel of God's presence saved the Israelites. (Isaiah 63:9) That angel is willing to be the only comrade having any influence with the young man.

But this wonderful champion and savior never comes forward unspoken of. He must be wooed forward by the same ardent stories of his redeeming and guiding glory as the preachers have told of Satan in his darkness. Step by step shall redemption draw nigh till the full-orbed splendor of love and peace and wisdom occupy the earth.

"For our Redeemer is strong; the Lord of hosts is His name; He shall thoroughly plead our cause, that He may give rest to the land."

At the first sound of your thought on the airs of silence, the angel moves forward as the blade of a grain steals up through the soils. At the first touch of your love, he pushes aside pain and trouble with a gentle heart sweet as a young blade of corn in the field. Emboldened by the hot sun and strong wind of your eager confidence, he masters the world for your sake. This is the Spirit. This is the only power there is or ever can be to make intemperance nothing whatever any more at all. The new Science teaches entirely of spiritual presence, spiritual power, spiritual possibilities. The ways of inert, incompetent matter are not mentioned in the new Science.

Inter-Ocean Newspaper, May 21, 1893

Lesson IX

Only One Power

Information taken from Review

May 28th [manuscript missing] calls the spiritual judgment of every mind the "woman." It calls the strong exhibition of good sense which every mind is capable of making, the "man." Wisdom sits enthroned in the heart. Bold expressions of wisdom "sit in the gates" of the world's cities. Whoever acts and speaks wisely listens to the gentle voice of the Spirit within. There is a great deal of folly and one-sidedness where the inner whispers are browbeaten into silence. All this mental and spiritual action shows itself out in the household and the business world. The household and the business world will never be balanced, delighting us with harmony and justice, till each mind listens to its spiritual wisdom. It has been promised that when our own mind listens to its true promptings and acts them out, almost in the twinkling of an eye, the mind of the whole world will listen and act wisely. For there is but one mind, and if one moves, all move. What one thinks and lives, all must think and live. This is true only of spiritual promptings. We cannot predicate anything of imaginary promptings: they seem to act, but do nothing. There really is but one power. That is Spirit. "There is none beside me."

LESSON X

RECOGNIZING OUR SPIRITUAL NATURE

Proverbs 31:10-31

The writer of Proverbs 31:10-31 is called Lemuel. Lemuel means "God with them." God is the spiritual nature of mind. Sometimes mind becomes aware of its spiritual nature as within itself, sometimes as without itself. Every mind that has become in any sense aware of its spiritual life is Lemuel. When mind recognizes its spiritual life it is marvelous how high above its human errors it swings itself and how, in spite of them, it is greatly blessed.

Read the story of Jacob if it seems to you as if you had committed so many transgressions against your highest self that you could never be blessed with the omnipotence of the guiding kindness. He took away his brother's spiritual birthright, yet looking upward he prospered. He "stole" his brother's heritage of spiritual imbuement, yet with his mind fixed on the rustling wings of the cherubim of peace and light, he grew strong and wise. He deceived his wife's father, yet, expecting the help of the unfailing God, he knew that the angel of defense tented wheresoever he slept. His mind was not wholly married to God. It was indeed unbendingly determined to keep sight and hearing of Spirit, but never melted into entire deference to Spirit. *"I will not let thee go except thou bless me"* (Genesis 32:26*), is the cry of a will always deflected from the meekness that could cry,* *"Nevertheless, not my will, but Thine be done"* (Matthew 26:39). Jacob fought hard with his own spiritual nature for a moiety (one of two equal parts) of what he might have had a universe full.

Was Called Emmanuel

The only yielding Jacob could do was to repent. He would not take the way of complete yielding to have all of God. He would not be bone of bone and life of life with Omnipotence through meekness. Yet he was blessed. It was Jesus who was kind through meekness, merged by meekness with the mighty Presence that fills heaven and earth. *"He did not strive nor cry"* (Matthew 12:19) for His greatness, yet He is "King of kings and Lord of lords." Therefore, He was called Emmanuel. Lemuel is a contraction of this name, suggestive more of one who is trying to come into union with the omnipotent Spirit of God than of one who has found it.

As these verses of Lemuel are the subject of to-day's lesson, we will follow this mind who realizes that there is a spiritual quickening within his reach which all the rubies of the Orient could not buy, yet which each man and woman of creation may have in limitless glory.

The spiritual life of the mind is often called the bride in sacred writings. *"The spirit and the bride say, Come"* (Revelation 22:17). It is sometimes called the wife, "The Lamb's wife." Intelligence may be strong and commanding, but while it is unvivified by the mysterious goodness of Spirit, it conveys to the world no bread and wine.

These verses go on to describe the wife-nature of God as manifest where intelligence has in meekness been lightened and brightened by its own Spirit. They describe how faithful and patient and wise a woman becomes in her home when her mind catches gleams of its own glorious powers. The outward home will symbolize the satisfied rest of intelligence that has been spiritualized. The clothing will typify the glistening garments of spiritual thoughts falling in beauty over the mind. The children will step forth fearlessly in honor and greatness to manifest the self-increasing and self-perpetuating power of mind made into Spirit.

Jesus Christ taught that each mind is in itself both God the Father and God the Mother. He demonstrated that the mind spiritualized makes a noble and glorified life. The life is the Son. Whoever has felt his mind entirely quickened by the

Spirit lives utterly; blameless. Those who struggle to lay hold upon the Spirit cannot live the life. They may feel great protection and accomplish even miracles, but there's a withered tendon somewhere which stands the waiting monument of something not yielded to Spirit. It is the disease or misfortune that Jacob's unyielded trait of character manifested as withered sinew. To them there is always a wrong seeming in the home.

"The virtuous wife who's price is above rubies" (verse 10), they cannot have till they have, *"trusted their heart in her"* (verse 11), the never-absent angel of God's presence. There are many ways of showing this trust in the angel of light accompanying each mind. Sometimes it is by keeping the strict letter of the covenant of peace. The last covenant which men are to make with the Almighty is the covenant of peace. They shall covenant for their life, and they shall do nothing for their life. The meek trust of mind in the Almighty Spirit would then make it impossible for a soldier or a policeman to be found guarding any city on earth. The city must not think it needs other defense of its life than God the Spirit. *"Except the Lord keep the city the watchman waketh in vain"* (Psalms 127:1). They who covenant the covenant of peace throw down defenses, throw down weapons of warfare, and let the hosts from on high disarm their enemies as the power of God, (looking through the irresistible eyes of Jesus) caused an army to fall prostrate.

The Covenant of Peace

In finding this "woman" of Proverbs, the covenant of peace must be yielded to in honor. We may not find the strength and prosperity of the spiritual nature of our own mind if we have covenanted for our health and prosperity to do nothing for them and then use the material methods signifying our persistent turning toward the unspiritual. We may find this priceless treasure of our own mind through making the covenant of peace. We may not lay hold upon it to carry out our wishes while we ignore the covenant of peace.

Jacob manufactured 14 years of time for himself through conniving to assist himself when his trust was pledged to the Jehovah of Isaac. Thus it was long years of hard labor for the possession of Rachel. Thus it was a night of hand-to-hand wrestling with the Spirit for its blessing till his thigh was unjointed.   Thus with us all when we take the words of the covenant and promise the trust of our heart in the Divine Presence and then do for our health and protection, our life and strength, exactly what the rest of the world are doing. We manufacture long vistas of time. We manufacture hard struggling for ourselves.

Though we are free to use the methods of the world, though they are not to be despised, yet covenanting to trust in the Spirit for our health, strength, prosperity, we cannot be mind-quickened by Spirit while we do use them. This is spoken of in a figure in the 10th and 11th verses of this 31st

Chapter. If we read it not as entirely referring to the shadow system of the universe, we shall feel illuminated to recognize that the "woman," or "bride," of the Scriptures is always the figure of our own spiritual power. If we "safely trust" it, we "have no lack of gain." If we perform with little bottles and pills for our bodily health, we have no heart; safely trusting in the word of God for our health. Fourteen years we may languish under our disease.

"Thy words were found and I did eat them," cannot be said of our health. It cannot be said of our prosperity, and we may languish under poverty 14 years for not safely trusting our heart in the Spirit of Goodness to work out our bountiful renewals.

If we read this set of Bible verses as the description of a good and strong housekeeper, we shall be dealing with the symbol instead of the spirit of them. *The letter killeth but the spirit giveth life* (II Corinthians 2:6), or quickeneth. There is but one spiritual meaning to them, and that is the spiritualization of our own intelligence till all outward things arrange themselves in harmony.

The 12th verse reads, *She doeth him good, and not evil, all the days of her life.* Take the meaning of this strongly into your heart. If a child dies, the loving God ever saw fit to take it to Himself. If the heart mourns it was not because of affliction that "she", the "mother" nature of God,

86

sent upon it. Her special and only wisdom is to give life and comfort to them that mourn. These trials are broken covenants showing outwardly; not actions of the Mother-God. If we will make these burdens of time, we may see them through. When the covenant of peace is kept, the angel shall stand with one foot on the sea and the other on the land (Revelation 10:2) and proclaim that time is no more. If the ways of time are offered us, we do not need to receive them.

The Ways of Time

The ways of time are the teachings of what shall come to us some day of health, strength, union with Spirit. The Spirit is here now. In Spirit what is waiting to be done? Nothing. Of this ma-jestic presence it is written: "It is finished;" "all is well." "Hands" are efficient thoughts. *"She worketh willingly with her hands"* (verse 13). Instantane-ous manifestation of good lies in the thoughts that our mind uses when it "safely trusts" this never-absent, never-failing Mother-God.

Mind is the father nature. Spirit is the mother nature. While we cannot show instantaneous good by our thoughts we have not found the Spirit. Our home is not right. From afar as it seems to us the *"merchant ships"* (verse 14) of prosperity come sailing when we keep our pledge to the Mother-God. They founder at sea, and we wail over our tedious years when we do not keep our covenant. All these things spoken of here in this Proverbs 31 come to us and our home by reason of some meek yielding of our will to the requests of the mother nature. Her ministry is unceasing. The night and the day alike find her bringing strength from afar and laying the treasures of all nations at our feet. There is nothing which she will not do; but there is one point we must yield which now we stick to as tenaciously as Jacob clung to his trickiness in carrying his points. What is it? With each one it is different. When each one of us yields our one peculiar trickiness or scheming to do our own way whether or not, the light and glory of this Presence will be revealed in all its effulgence. There is only one point to yield. It is a very simple one — so easy perhaps for your neighbor that he never thinks of willfulness on that line. And his is so easy for you that you have never been aware of caring an iota to speak or act or think as he does. One person said he must be judged as having only so much of the Spirit of God in him as kept him from swearing. Another said he must be judged as having only so much of the Spirit of God in him as his generosity indicated. The first man liked to swear. The second man liked to hoard his money. Each one detected in his one trait a willful wandering from the Spirit, a refusal to let the Divine nature entirely into his mind premises.

Union with the Divine

Great blessings may accompany a character through all the pilgrimage we call earthly, but the greatly desired union with the divine is waiting for the keeping of that covenant which those who would quicken their mind with spiritual power have made. To each one, the verdict shall be: *"Thou excellest them all"* (verse 29). This covenant is sometimes called "trust in the Lord." It is sometimes called "rest in the Lord." Jacob would have been blessed without such terrible efforts. He thought it was his scheming efforts that brought him his blessings. We do not need to scramble and jump and dive for what the Spirit will bestow just for our trusting or resting in her. If we have said, "I will let Thee lead me," let us love the way we are led. When a hard affliction comes to us, it is the great bell of kindness ringing out the fruits and history of some breaking of that promise we once uttered: "I will trust Thee." "I will let Thee lead me." The tongue of the Spirit speaks mighty low to the heart while the misery of conniving to do our own way for health or life or strength or prosperity is at its full.

"The law of kindness is in her tongue" (verse 26). We need not look to the external home for our spiritual rest. Looking to the Spirit of our own mind and giving it to the government of our whole thoughts will make the external home right.

We need not look to men or women or children or successes or honors for our spiritual joy. Looking to the spiritual quality of our own mind and giving it absolute government over our affairs will make men and women and children do what is right to us. But there is one thing which must be attended to first — one idea of the Spirit and of the life we must yield up. When we make up our mind what external habit we are keeping up, which we have felt bent upon carrying out, but with which now we will have no more dealings, the great bell of God is ringing that some melting of a mental error into the molten sea of goodness has begun. Not until we are ready to deal with this external habit exactly right, is the sound of the voice of the Spirit heard in showing us the fulfillment of our heart's fondest wish, for at this point, the seeming divergence of mind and Spirit is made.

Miracles Will Be Wrought

The works of the Spirit in your mind shall praise you in the gates when you hold not out in willful persistence anymore at all. In all other points of your life you may not touch the external. There will be miracles wrought for you.

In one point you must touch the external and give up your action. This lesson tells entirely of spiritualizing intelligence. It calls intelligence the husband or father quality of each mind, and calls spiritual thought the wife or mother quality of each mind. It shows that home and prosperity and health and knowledge will be sure to arrange themselves in beautiful harmony when we give the spiritual nature of our own mind its rights with our thoughts. It teaches that a covenant must be entered into by our own mind with our own Spirit, and kept unflinchingly. We must covenant with the Spirit in us to do all things and we will do nothing. So what is left for the husband quality or mind nature to do by this, (Proverbs 31:10-31)? All is done by the Holy Spirit or mother quality of your mind except one thing, and that is, cutting off your favorite material performance. Maybe you have a habit of grieving. It is bone of your bone and flesh of your flesh. Deliberately cut it off. Maybe you have a habit of complaining. It is bone of your bone and flesh of your flesh. Cut it off by your own sword.

The mind nature sits at the world's gates and seems to do all things, but it is the Spirit back of and running through the mind which gives life and zest and substance to thoughts and words and actions. *"Her husband is known in the gates when he sitteth among the elders of the land"*(verse 23). Mind seems to receive all the honors; but only the honor gathered by the Spirit of mind is real; all else is sham. The Spirit never deals with shams or unrealities. The mind seems to deal with them until it is given utterly to Spirit. Mind, to be utterly spiritualized, must look squarely at what seems to it to be a real tie, but what is not spiritually true, and cut it. Yet this cutting off, which seems to be action, is still giving the spiritual nature active sway. It is cessation from action which seems to require effort of will.

Inter-Ocean Newspaper, June 4, 1893

LESSON XI

INTUITION

Ezekiel 8:2-3, 9:3-6, 11

Ezekiel's visions were not wholly clear to himself. He thought this one meant the destruction of the people by five angels sent forth from heaven to express the wrath of God. The vision represents the fulfillment of the senses under the belief that their being is limited to material things. There are said to be five limited senses. There is a sixth, called intuition, which no man ever limited. He might say it was absent from him, or that if he obeyed it he would never get into trouble, but not a man on the planet ever said it made mistakes for him or, if listened to, was lacking in power. This sense is symbolized by the man clothed in linen who marks the foreheads and whose mark saves life.

Ezekiel's lesson in the life-increasing power of the intuitive sense, as expressed in the 9th Chapter, is identical in substance with that of Solomon, in the 5th Chapter of Ecclesiastes. An undivided state of mind on any theme brings revelations. Ezekiel had felt that sense indulgence was spoiling Israel and Judah. He believed the senses were running riot after material things and that this ought to be stopped. He thought the Spirit was so angry and revengeful because of the efforts of the senses to find satisfaction in the lines ordained to them, that it would slay all who had given their senses the liberty to search materiality to the utmost. So he had a vision personifying each of his own feelings.

Dreams and Their Cause

Solomon tells us that dreams come from a multitude of business. Ezekiel's mind was filled with his manifold anxieties about Israel and Judah. If any man or woman begins to absorb himself in worry about daily matters, fearing he is doing wrong, after a while, some sorrowful-faced being will come in his dreams and look reproachfully at him. Or, if it is the prevailing undercurrent of his mind that something is going wrong against him, a figure of chaos will be pictured. Solomon, therefore, says it is greatly advantageous when in a place of worship, where solemn and high themes have been brought forth, that we keep our thoughts very still and let the great thought in the church reveal its blessing to us. We are capable of receiving anything if we are open to it. *"Be more ready to hear than to give the sacrifice"* (Ecclesiastes 5:1).

"God is in heaven, and thou upon earth: there-fore let thy words be few" (Ecclesiastes 5:2). To Solomon, his own inspirations were hardly more clear than were Ezekiel's to him. He puts God afar off, and man is made to inhabit a God-deserted earth. But inspiration means that when the mind thinks as God thinks, all is harmony and praise and approval. One who feels it his duty to go and tell a man his faults is not looking at the man as God looks at him. He had better "let his words be few" till he sees his neighbor as God sees him. An angel who looks reproachful came not from God.

Israel and Judah

Ezekiel, speaking of Israel and Judah, and Solomon, speaking of church worshippers, show that they have watched the externals of man's life till they have completely identified themselves with its psychology. But visions always have lofty purports, and inspirations to write have their own purposes, regardless of the personal bents of their writers' minds. Ezekiel's vision of the self-destructiveness of the five senses carries the irre-sistible idea that it is not by giving the senses their liberty, but by limiting them in dealing with matter, that there is, finally, death. The eyes have been called the windows of the soul. If soul is God, what shall hinder it from looking through and beyond material things into the remotest distances of unbounded heaven? Nothing, but, limiting it by the belief that it can see only material things.

Each of us has enough power of soul to strengthen his vision to unimaginable borders. So with each sense. The soul-strength that lies back of the five senses is the spring of living power within, which has no limit to its supplies. Jesus was a poor carpenter's son, born in a manger, and thus had no better material chances for knowing how to be greater or wiser or abler than his fellow beings. But look at the increasing power in the world which was his because he uncovered the inner well of power. And this same power is available to all who cast off the stones and sticks of tradition concerning sense limitation. He gave the senses all rights. He made them reach in undeflected strength through matter, taking matter's folded particles along on their rays, and spreading it thinner than the air of clearest noonday. How, then, could he help seeing *"the flesh profiteth nothing"* (John 6:63)? Watching the march of his unchecked faculties, we cannot fail to see that all material things are only beliefs in sense limitations. Take off the rein holding the five senses to one province only (that of pure materiality) and all Spirit will be visible. This is the teaching of the sixth sense, when it is listened to.

Intuition the Head

Intuition is the head of the angel of power within us. It is eternal right judgment. Its seat is in the forehead, where we see it symbolized. All the other parts of the body act in harmony with it when it has been listened to till its mark is visible.

Each limb stands for a sense whose province is limited by believing in its power of shortness to act. But *"God's arm is not shortened that it cannot save"* (Isaiah 59:1) — and God is the soul within us. To know this is to start the five senses out on their deathless journeys of strength and to enthrone judgment in the forehead.

Should one, like Ezekiel, attempt to symbolize his despair of finding satisfaction for the senses in the materiality to which they have been limited, he would picture it as people being slain with knives carried by five angels. Solomon would see it as a fool chattering vanity till there was nothing left of him. To see it with the mark of the sixth angel upon the forehead is to see the old province of the senses extending from the soul within, taking matter out of their wings, unfolding and unrolling till what is beyond matter is joyfully touched.

We find that the intelligence of soul is all that is real in sight, hearing, feeling, and tasting. Soul knows no particles of matter. Our knowing this about the soul illuminates and transfigures our presence. Knowing it and rejoicing in it fixes the light of transfiguration so that there is no more of the material in us or by us forever. The sixth doctrine concerning God that has come to the race finds that there is nothing to hate; finds there is no sickness; finds there is no crime, no pain.

Pushing through these, and taking them out on the wings of the soul which has no longer any speech or language telling of error and limitation, pain and disease are discovered to be only the result of claiming that matter has owned sensation when, in reality, sensation belongs entirely to the Spirit. We falter no more in fear before angels. Our converse is like theirs — all, all approval. *"Say not thou before the angel that it was an error"* (Ecclesiastes 5:6). Whatever we name the mighty energy within us, with its power to fill the universe — whether soul, mind, spirit, God, angel, Buddha, Jesus Christ — makes no difference. Our belief in its omnipotence will give it free spring forward through creation, as the power of Jesus is now making itself felt. Whoever feels the truth of this is already open to give forth and to receive, as by a process of breathing, his own power with which he has forever been vested. This power may show forth one way in one character and other way in another. One student, when she heard of it, discovered for the first time that she had never had any perspective in objects before her vision. All things had always seemed to her flat and pressed close to her sight. They soon began to remove into a more usual perspective.

Our Limited Perspective

As Chinese paintings discover to us that this race has no sense of perspective, so our pains and our troubles show what limited perspectives we have allowed ourselves. To the young girl who had never seen buildings except as flat, upright planes close at hand, their removal was delightful freedom. For all the liberated "spirits in prison," as Paul called those who were much under tradition and materiality, there is sweet reviving peace.

"Let us fly the boundaries of the senses. Let us live the free, unhurt life of the soul."

So shall matter be removed and cast into the molten sea of that world of the blest for which every heart panteth as the hart after the water brooks.

"The sleep of the laboring man is sweet, whether he eat little or much" (Ecclesiastes 5:12), writes Solomon, explaining that *"he that loveth silver shall not be satisfied with silver, nor he that loveth abundance (of any material) with increase"* (Ecclesiastes 5:10). There is a labor that is bread and meat to man, and that is the labor to give all his faculties into the keeping of his own soul. Then he seems to fast but in reality he is filled and satisfied. His sleep is long and profound that he may be free from the memory of material things and experience only the sweet, untrammeled soul life.

Inter-Ocean Newspaper, June 11, 1893

LESSON XII

The Power of Faith

Malachi

"Faith is the one open road between gods and men." No matter how many prayers you repeat, if in your heart there is timidity and doubt as to whether an answer will be given, then there will be no manifestation of divine power. If only there is faith, then, laying aside all questions about the gods, the god in your own soul will be manifested in power. Though we ask for nothing more than a sardine's head, its reception depends upon our faith, and the divinity within our soul is called out by this earnest faith.

Exercise of Thankfulness

"An unbeliever might say, 'so then to speak of receiving divine help for the cure of disease is really to speak of man's own state of mind as the cause of his recovery; the power of the gods has nothing to do with it.' We must reply that this state of mind is true faith, and therein is the wonderful principle of the working together of gods and men. He that has life in himself so as to call out the life of the universe readily obtains divine aid."

These words are from a Buddhist priest's sermon. Algazel, the Mohammedan, called the faith of a soul in the working nearness of the Divine Being the point of contact between God and man. How to get this faith they none of them tell. He who came nearest to stating a plan of action or reasoning that would bring forth from the sealed-up soul its own working faith was the Shinto Kuro-zumi, in his lessons on cheerfulness and thankfulness. We can all start out, with being thankful that we have within us, sealed though it may be from practical efficiency, this potential factor of existence. We can be thankful that it is our own point of contact with the omnipotent God.

The exercise of thankfulness in even the smallest degree will awaken something like ardent expectancy of coming good. It will brighten the eye with new intelligence. It is our privilege to multiply gratitude to the state of ecstasy — entranced expectation of good — which is living faith. We may expect then anything we ask for. Nothing is scorned by the principle of giving.

On the plane where our wants are named, the divine light symbolizes itself. The Buddhist priest mentioned a sardine's head. He received it. The missionaries mentioned money. They got it. The general mentioned reinforcements. He got them.

The mother mentioned bread and clothes. They came by express. The father spoke of some evidence that his beloved daughter had not died. Her smiling face greeted him on the dusty road. The young preacher asked for illumination. His heart and face were glorified. The Jews of old mentioned foreknowledge of the time of the end of Bible history and Bible prophecy. They received Malachi.

Here, in Malachi, we may read the history of religion and its final character, as it closes down over the destinies of man and nature. It is the Jacob of the line of doctrine. It undermines and supplants science, art, politics, commerce, mechanics, trade, scholarship, everything which is the Esau of human life.

"I loved Jacob, and I hated Esau," saith the Lord, "and I laid his mountains and his heritage waste..." (Malachi 1:2-3) *"The Lord will cut off... the master and the scholar..."* (Malachi 2:12) *"And I will be a swift witness ... against those that oppress the hireling in his wages, the widow, and the fatherless, and turn aside the stranger from his right, and fear not me"* (Malachi 3:5).

It is Esau who, by right of pre-emption, seems to have the earth for his heritage. Materiality — with its terrible methods of "first come, first served," "to the victor belongs the spoils," "that a rose may breathe its breath something must die," "business is business," warfare and money dealings — seems to own the world. But Jacob, the second thought, the promised son, with his faults fallen away, is the spirituality which, creeping and running and flying through the ages, finally lays hold upon all things.

Her Faith Self-Sufficient

As Jacob needed not to resort to stratagem to own the birthright and land of Abraham, so religion need never have stooped to artifice to have captured the mountains and valleys of earth with all the inhabitants thereof. Her faith was self-sufficient and had promised her all things.

As Jacob made of himself an exile and made his years long in the land of sorrow and affliction, so has religion been long exiled by her priests, and her people have eaten the bread of shame and humiliation, patience and perseverance, which were not native to them. But at the core, religion itself has always been right. It has had the right Jacob soul in its reverse power of prevailing with God. Roused to its best, it has always wrought out life where materiality's best was death. Religion at its best is faith in the good, ignoring the evil; faith in life and peace, renouncing death and discord. *"My covenant with him was of life and peace"*(Malachi 2:5).

Esau resented Jacob's artifices. He despised him for them. Jacob himself was ashamed of them, and afraid because of them, but he never repented; he died as flesh and came forth as 12 sons who purified their hearts for the descent of Messiah. So religion has had to hang her head because of her history. She has died through her formalism, given the world her 12 lessons, and now, in the spirit and life of the new light breaking through the whole mind of man, comes suddenly into her temple as God.

"But who may abide the day of his coming, and who shall stand when he appeareth" (Malachi 3:2)? Those who profess that their faith has been sufficiently aroused to carry them through human hardship without turning them to ashes, may find that, like Jacob, they have been taking it upon themselves to assist the Almighty in managing their estate. They may find that their patient waiting and years of persevering labor are only religious subterfuge to hide their non-practice of faith.

When the law came suddenly into the temple, it found the doctrine of patience made a spiritual virtue. Then the law took the *"fuller's soap"* (Malachi 3:2) of irrefutable arguments and washed down that sanctimonious cuticle to the plane of exposure where it was manifest that as God never has to be patient, so man that is born of God has no call to patient endurance. It showed the "Sons of Levi" (ministers of religion) that suffering in any form is clear evidence of faith sealed in, not set free. It took them at their own word that the divinity within all men is right faith. Divinity is God. Thus faith is God. God has not to labor with persevering patience through years of disappointing delays; therefore faith knows nothing of disappointing delays. The inference is clear. They who wait and labor through disappointing delays have not exercised faith. It has looked like it, but it was only a simulacrum (likeness) of faith, a hiding of their daily habit of conniving and planning what to do next in order to come out prosperous.

Burned with the Fires of Truth

"Both the master and the scholar" (Malachi 2:12) in this process of sealing up shall be cut off. All that is not ardent expectation of good, so joyous that it exposes everything above mentioned in an instant, is dead. It is to be burned with the *"refiner's fire"* (Malachi 3:2) of straight questions.

Read all of Malachi instead of the few verses selected as today's lesson. Take for its key, Esau for materiality and Jacob for spirituality. Or, the world's methods and religious methods. Look up Jacob's history which describes the way of the ministers of religion through the ages. You will see that the perfectly spiritual doctrine calls much of the preaching which passes for high piety, direct robbery from God. *"Will a man rob God? Yet ye have robbed me"* (Malachi 3:8).

"Cursed be the deceiver which sacrificeth unto the Lord a corrupt thing" (Malachi 1:14). *"Ye have brought that which was torn and lame, and the sick"* (Malachi 1:13). Has it not been counted as fine religion for the paralytic, rheumatic, consumptive and palsied to declare that they were chosen of the Lord of Hosts to wear the gifts of His afflictions? And, being resigned to His will that they should be thus torn and lame and sick, have

they not been considered shining lights of right-eousness? But the finest fires of truth burn away this chaff of excess. It is robbery of God to take or keep from him the honor of having made all things out of His own unalterable beauty. *"I am God; I change not"* (Malachi 3:6). It is offering Him the results of false swearing to give Him the credit of voluntarily putting palsy or blindness upon His own substance. *"I will be a swift witness against false swearers"* (Malachi 3:5).

Each coarse and worldly allusion, as "sorcery, adultery, oppression" and the like, can be pushed clear on to the plains of religious professions. Sorcery is idolatry. It is throwing chemical compounds together, and burning and melting material ingredients to make medicines for curing the people, when there is no cure except in knowledge of truth. It is weaving and sewing cloths and straws together for clothing, when the highest truth told of the spirit and its white living faith would show how all are to be clothed by the Spirit of God. It is buying cheap and selling dear that prosperity may satisfy our life, when we are especially taught not to look at such methods, for "prosperity, we know, is of thee alone."

Who are greater adulterers than those who, having proclaimed that *"we have all one father, and one God created us"* (Malachi 2:10), proceed to deal treacherously against that principle by describing their vile imaginations against the sons and daughters of God and punishing them as truth and reality? According to the closing prophecy of that Malachi who answered the prayer of the Jews concerning knowledge of things to be in these days, it is "sorcery and adultery" on our part to yield a single iota of power to materiality. It is "oppression" to listen to the doctrine of delay of prosperity. All outward and physical *"sorcery, adultery, oppression"* (Malachi 3:5) had their rise in mental yielding to the preaching of appearances. Appearance is not reality.

What Is Reality?

What is reality? Spirit of joy manifest. Spirit of peace manifest. Spirit of unalterable beauty manifest. There is no worry or discord except in the imagination of the mind that there are ways to live independently of Spirit; ways to be healed by materiality; ways to be wise except by knowledge of Spirit. These imaginations are to be suddenly annihilated by the Lord when we are seeking, coming suddenly into our midst, to greet face to face the teaching that God is slow and lets wickedness prosper above spiritual confidence. *"Your words have been stout against me. Ye had said, 'What profit is it that we have kept his ordinances?' We call the proud happy. Yea, they that tempt God are even delivered"* (Malachi 3:13-15).

In offering up the tithes of doctrine, we have robbed God of the honor of giving wisdom to all men liberally and of upholding them in impartial measure. We have taken from Him His place in the universe by our belief in the reality of Esau.

With mind open to what is being taught of the rights of Esau, we have let in the doctrine of the absence of good as Spirit and of the presence of good as pottage, till we are seemingly governed by bad. *"Prone to err as the sparks to fly upward" (Job 5:7).* *"Know ye not, that to whom ye yield yourselves servants to obey, his servants ye are to whom ye obey"* (Romans 6:16).

One can bare his forehead to wait for condemnation or complaints or temptations of himself till he is entirely possessed by self-depreciation. Has he not thus robbed God of the infinite praise of his beautiful character which God is always giving? Then, being driven by self-depreciation, if he hastens to act out stealing and lying and cheating — which only come from letting into the mind *"words of the priests' lips who keep not knowledge"* (Malachi 2:7), what other actions could be expected to manifest themselves from being mentally open to the doctrine of iniquity? He has not inherited iniquity. *"Have we not all one father? Hath not one God created us"* (Malachi 2:10)?

A child was discovered talking in a foreign language which its parents and its teachers could not speak or understand. A traveler from a land across the sea understood her and conversed with her. Did she inherit the language? Was it not that her open mind listened to the finer tones of another way of telling the stories of daily life than her parents used?

The Lord, or the Science of Spirit, hath come into His temple now. He tells a story of God's thoughts of man so unlike the language of the schools and the church, that schools and church, like the parents of that child, think there is something wrong, something daft or imbecile in the language

But they that have the high praises of the lover of the universe *"speak often one to another"* (Malachi 3:16), *"and they shall be mine, saith the Lord of Hosts, in that day when I make up my jewels, and I will spare them"* (from pain and sickness and ignorance and poverty and feebleness) *"as a man spareth his own son that serveth him"* (Malachi 3:17). They that hear this language know that if there is any defeat apparent in them, it is because they need to turn a still more open ear to the voice of praise of themselves that chants its bright music through the coarse descriptions of their imperfections. Then upon them shall *"the sun of righteousness arise with healing in his wings"* (Malachi 4:2).

One Open Road

Baring the forehead to the immortal breezes of the truth as it is now being wafted from zone to zone, who hears his petitions condemned as too material, too earthly, too sordid? Does he not rather hear: *"Whatsoever ye shall ask, believing, ye shall receive"* (Matthew 21:22). Does he not feel the arm of infinite kindness stretching down to bear him up into answered prayers?

How can he keep from singing of the wonderful God who has come now *"opening the windows of heaven, and pouring out blessings so that there is not room enough to receive them"*(Malachi 3:10).

The one open road between God and man is made. Over its comforting substance goes the soul of man fearlessly into the soul that is God. And into the sealed places where faith has been closed all the three days since our healer was with us, comes God in His goodness and glory. Religion, the prevailer with omnipotence, burned of her robberies of spirit by the pure fires of science, brings now all the tithes into the storehouse. She yields no power or place to matter. She looks into the Spirit for all things. Jacob has undermined and supplanted Esau. Religious man, knowing only God, has conquered.

Inter-Ocean Newspaper, June 18, 1893

LESSON XIII

REVIEW OF THE SECOND QUARTER

1893

Kossuth said that when, as governor of Hungary, he was at times bound to his bed by sickness, he would say to his body, "Be well!" and it would obey. He did not have to exercise any force of will to bring his body into health; it responded to his commands as a good servant answers the bell. Kossuth took a course with his body quite opposite to that which the generality of mankind takes; his body obeyed him — he did not obey his body.

The dominion of the mind, without exercise of the effort of the will beyond the province of choice, may be extended to the whole territory of man's affairs. He may enlarge his borders of dictatorship to all the conditions he wishes to manage till the winds and waves obey him, and not he them. At first when man, as mind, begins to dictate to his body, he conveys so much timidity and non-

113

expectancy of obedience that the body, like an impatient domestic, laughs him in the face and does the straight opposite of the command. But if man, as mind, will simply state his orders over again without effort, and again if he will state them, being the natural governor, he will directly be obeyed.

We as Mind, are Kings

So also affairs which, like Kossuth's body run painfully, may first grin their disobedience in our sight. But having been once vested with authority, we have authority forever and are bound to be respected by our natural servants. "There's such divinity doth hedge a king." (William Shakespeare, Hamlet IV:v) And we, as mind, are kings. The affairs that have fallen to our lot are our natural servitors. Try giving orders to your affairs. Do not stop telling them how they must arrange themselves because they don't arrange instantly. If it seems to take time and you do not want it to take time to bring matters around to suit yourself, turn to time and tell it to stand aside for you. Enlarge the borders of your jurisdiction to extend over time till it is no more.

John, the Seer, saw an angel, with one foot on the sea and one on the land (Revelation 10:2), proclaiming that time should be no more. An angel is a noble idea. Your command from the kingly standpoint is an angel. Time is as much your servant as your body is.

The talking of all things for your obedient servants in this way may be your only way to manifest the stupendous doctrine of the "I AM" which is symbolized by the man-child that is to rule all nations (Revelation 12). Some go into their reign over their own earth by dictating like masters; others, by the priestly line of saying that God is all, and therefore all is well. Since appearances terribly dispute that all is God or all is well, the kingly position of compelling things accomplishes the same results as either the meek acquiescence of the priestly process or the philosophic reasoning out of things.   The result is the same, namely, identification of the self with the "I AM" at the center.

When any mind gets manifest mastery over everything without striving with it by any manner whatsoever, the manifestation of that mastery is resurrection of Jesus Christ — God-man. Whatsoever conditions are managed by material struggles, such management is not resurrection of Jesus Christ.

The lesson of April 2nd, described the uprising of the body of Jesus Christ at the command of his mind, without the intervention or assistance of physical means. He rose that we might rise. He ascended into the throne by the kingly line of government. *"The government was on his shoulders"* (Isaiah 9:6). He ascended into his throne by the priestly line of meek acquiescence. *"I am meek and lowly of heart"* (Matthew 11:29). *"Thy will be done"*

(Matthew 6:10). He ascended into his throne by the philosopher's reasonable logic. *"He that receiveth you receiveth me, and he that receiveth me receiveth him that sent me"* (John 13:20). *"I am in the Father and the Father in me"* (John 14:11). *"The Father in me and I in you"* (John 14:20). Nothing could ever keep things in heaven, on earth, and under the earth from bending the knee to such threefold assumption of prerogatives.

Resurrection Is Manifesting

When our life faces us and seems ungainly, is it in truth our life that faces us, or what we have not believed about resurrection that is manifesting? We are told to manifest glory, immortality, health, dominion, joy, satisfaction. These and much more have been our inheritance from divinity since ever from divinity we came forth.

"Not in entire forgetfulness,

And not in utter nakedness,

But trailing clouds of glory do we come,

From God who is our home."

The lesson of April 9th shows that by the line of profound meekness, the entrance into great prosperity is generally attended with what seems like afflictions. Job at first was so meek that he boasted of never having meddled with things too high for him. He ended by absorbing the whole God of omnipresence, omnipotence, omniscience. He found the whole Father in himself exactly as Jesus found the whole Father in himself and was in the most abject starvation till he rose to know the Almighty himself. He took counsel with everybody who came to him, and followed where they led, like a lamb to the slaughter, till they touched his soul with the strings of belief in its sinfulness.

Then his soul ascended into its place and boldly proclaimed its spotless integrity. The spotless God created the soul of His own substance. Meekness always leads to knowledge of this. Sooner or later, where the heart has always yielded and conceded to others believed to be wiser-thinking in meekness that the great good would be wrought out by following wiser leads — the soul springs forth as king.

If you have yielded and conceded to those whom you have thought wiser than yourself, hoping ever that the greatest good to your cause, or your children, or your country would be subserved thereby, there will come a day when some overpowering good will spring forth for you. Do you remember the blind man who had always tried everything everybody told him, thinking surely they knew and would help him, how one glorious morning (so glorious that he could only fall on his face and rise shouting for joy whenever he remembered it) there came one final test of his meekness — he must run through a jeering crowd with his eyes covered with wet clay, which a lowly carpenter's son had told him would cure him! (John 9)

This lesson reads: "Ah! gentle heart, hoping and trusting and willing, one final test of meekness and life shall be worthwhile for you."

April 16th, speaks exactly what Jesus meant by *"the kingdom of God cometh not with observation"* (Luke 17:20). Job went forward and backward, to the right hand and to the left, hoping to see the divine kindness at its performance of melting his mountain of misery, but he could only know that there was no doubt about his coming out refined as gold by the fires, fair as the sunny waters of Uz, when shadows of weeping were past.

Grander Faith

Through all his life he had held on faithfully to his religious convictions. As he held them, they dissolved and showed him his capability for a finer, a grander faith. He reasoned with the Almighty with the elevated consciousness of conversing with an intelligence that could understand his deepest meanings. Not an ameliorating sentence, not a comforting circumstance came into sight or hearing or touch; yet he knew that the crystallized mountain of anguish, that had grown up so high that no sunshine could reach him because of it, was being destroyed, dissolved, was vanishing into thinness like mist. In the midst of the hardness, the darkest troubles, the noblest thoughts of God we have held are then working their swiftest.

As face-to-face talk with God is converse with high counsel which brings out our wisdom, so likewise it brings out health, and so in like manner it brings out peace. Reasoning with the Almighty is the scientific way of undermining evil. A great disease will dissolve and vanish for one who reasons with the Almighty as a man talketh with his brother.

Good reasoning will soon put any man where he will see that the Almighty has not set himself to contend against him. It will show him that the Almighty holds no grudge against him; that the Almighty remembers no sin he ever committed. He will see that his own thought that he has done something wrong is all there is between him and healing. When this vision of truth dawns on him, he knows his disease is in process of disintegrating. It looks as hard and hurts as hard as before, but it has not the same clutch on him. It is receding.

This same is true of the mountain of sorrow that piles itself so high before some lives. The same is true of the mass of misfortune that suddenly accumulates in the pathway of some people. Job had them all. But he knew they were being removed by some infinite tenderness. It was the natural working power of his own reasonings that was bringing the good day forward through the darkness of his present. There came a moment when he rose to understand that his good deeds were as much his imaginings as his evil ones. There was neither evil nor good between him and his God. Then peace came.

There is nothing between you and your God. You need not imagine you have either done wrong to have set Him against you, or right to have caused Him to favor you. Rest your heart in this knowledge. It is the philosopher's stone after which the ages have sought.

Lesson of Job's Life

April 23rd continued the lesson of Job's life. It brought out the action of the law upon people who believe so strongly in evil that they are ready to pounce upon the very Christ himself with accusations of his being a publican, a liar, and a Sabbath breaker. Just as meek Job is shouting his joyful discovery that God is the Father in him, and he is master over death and misfortune by his own divinity, his friends, who think it is sacrilege to find God the "I AM" of their mind, feel that they have not hurt Job by their condemnations. He is rising into prosperity and spiritual illumination by the pathway of blasphemy! They are not able to explain what seems to them to be the success of the wicked. It is a lesson which glows and glistens with the doctrine of giving every man freedom to speak of God as he pleases and in what manner his soul by nature breaks forth with kindly encouragement; never reproachfully. If a man chooses to rise to his kingship by reasonings, let him. If he chooses to rise into his dominion by meekness, let him.

One way which has been tried for ages and ages has only brought it about that the greatest claim among us is that of poverty and despair. It is the way taken by Job's friends. It is the way of reproach and accusation and fear of blasphemy. "God is so wise, yet He has never seen me as a wicked man or a sinner; why should you see me so?" Wonder the Jobs of this life as it seems.

Prosperity and healing have never come in on the roadbeds of reproach. They have come in on the lines of "God knows I am right in giving Him credit for having made every soul wise and good and one with His own soul, inseparable, indivisible. I must remove my reproach which makes me see them otherwise." The first thought with which to regard mankind, whether one alone or many together, is, "I remove my reproach."

April 30th lesson reiterates the old, old assurance, that every manifestation of Being in the universe is so filled with divine spiritual fire that it has a voice to teach us what is our very best and safest plan of action for every moment. It is foolish to ignore such a principle. It declares that to receive 50 ideas and keep them is invigorating and empowering.

Mankind has practiced sleeping little and on hard beds, eating coarsely, fighting and wrestling to increase the strength and size of muscles and joints. All the results of this process fall far short of the quality of strength which a few noble sentiments can build. Now and then people have stumbled upon some strengthening propositions and made themselves famous. They were not at all brilliant or promising as children. If their parents had trained them with dumbbells and boxing gloves to improve their vigor, it would not have availed like that idea with which they were stimulated. There was a young lad impressed with the German maxim that if we learn something new every day and do not know we have learned it, we are nothing advantaged; but if we learn something new and know that we have learned it, we have been advantaged. So he proceeded till he knew six languages grammatically. He was far from intelligent as the world speaks of brightness.

Strength a Spiritual Infusion

Many spiritually-minded people who have no occasion whatever to exhibit ability to lift or handle heavy objects of daily use would, if occasion should arise, astonish practiced workmen with their power to do so. Strength is a spiritual infusion. There is no materiality about it. Strength infuses itself through ideas. "I am strong" is the express-man's idea. It is the voice of the Spirit in him. There is an idea now being accepted which is, in reality, from the Spirit, though its owners do not say so. It is that we have another faculty than those in use. By cultivating it we shall be able to see and understand more about things than we would know about the things themselves if we studied them for ages. In Swedenborg, this faculty was aroused to some extent, and he is now spoken of in Stockholm as mystical and not canny. They cannot yet see that when he could easily tell what was going on in Gottenberg as he sat in his library at Stockholm, he had only called up a universal gift. This unused power discovers the "thought" [sic] of all things.

May 7th gave some very practical hints for people who have believed in those ideas that have made poverty for them, and for those who have held notions that made them labor like dogs for their living, not because they had volunteered to go into the harness, but because they were forced to. It did not hesitate to inform us that denying the ideas of the world gives length of days and great freedom of life. Deny everything you hear except that which is exactly what your highest conception of God agrees with. Consider this motto, "Learn to labor and to wait." Deny that it is a real principle to go by. Does God have to learn to labor and to wait?

May 14th discusses the power of the word. By word is not meant the writings of Scripture, but the everyday words of every man's mouth. "A man shall be satisfied by the fruit of his mouth" (Proverbs 18:20) is the key text of the chapter. Every word comes to its full fruitage. We say carelessly, "That is the worst thing I ever saw." Now it is not the worst, but our words hurry around the universe to hunt up something worse than anything we have ever yet seen so that we may be satisfied at seeing our words come to pass.

Science of Interpretation

Everything we say tries to make us out truth-tellers by bringing our sayings to pass. We say, "She is the best singer I ever listened to." So these words go swiftly around seeking someone to light on that will be truly the best we ever heard. Sarah Bernhardt had such a passion for being called eccentric that when in Copenhagen at a hotel a few yards from the Royal Theatre, she had the street sprinkled with salt, and rode in a sleigh to the theatre, though it was in August. She got full satisfaction of her spoken idea concerning her own eccentricity there, for they thought she was mad — a lunatic. None is more eccentric than a lunatic. "He is a great fool!" we say. He is not a fool, but our faithful words find somebody who is, and we get into a predicament through the actions of the new fool our hearty little speech brought to us. *"For the lightest word ye shall give account"* (Matthew 12:36). The new science which interprets the Bible teachings in this way gives special lessons in erasing out of life's pathway words and their hastening fulfillments.

May 21st gave each one of us the key to his own character and prospects. One man lives by his sentimental feelings. He gives way to pleasure at good news and to depression at bad news. Success elates him. Disappointment sickens him. Such a man grows old young. His body becomes mealy and has no fiber.

Another man gives way to appetite of some kind. He imagines things that would gratify him and finds them out. He also shows old age young. There is no eternal substance, no abiding fiber, in physical appetites or sentimental impulses.

If a man lives, by his judgment, he feeds on an invigorating and renewing meat. At 65, his judgment is powerful. He may be just in readiness for the important post of ambassador to a great foreign court. He was no more gifted to set out with than certain others who were his classmates in boyhood. The difference is in the mental food they swallowed afterward.

No amount of smoothing the outer pathway of one man, or wrenching drinks and breads from another will invigorate or rejuvenate them. *"The flesh* (or external performances) *profiteth nothing"* (John 6:63). Let them hear the doctrine of Jesus that points to the divinity within them. Their spiritual ears will prick like the ears of the war horse when he hears the sound of the battle from afar. Nothing is so worthwhile as the doctrine of Jesus that imaginations of pleasure and pain are vanity — delusion. There is something that is true! It takes away both sentimental sniveling and smiling, and craving appetites, at once.

The new moralists and temperance workers will deal entirely with that doctrine. They won't hide the rum, for their converts couldn't be tempted thereby. Can God be tempted to drunkenness? They will speak to the God in man and *he "whose right it is" to reign shall come forth.* (Ezekiel 21:27)

Only One Power

May 28th [manuscript missing] calls the spiritual judgment of every mind the "woman." It calls the strong exhibition of good sense which every mind is capable of making, the "man." Wisdom sits enthroned in the heart. Bold expressions of wisdom "sit in the gates" of the world's cities. Whoever acts and speaks wisely listens to the gentle voice of the Spirit within. There is a great deal of folly and one-sidedness where the inner whispers are browbeaten into silence. All this mental and spiritual action shows itself out in the household and the business world. The household and the business world will never be balanced, delighting us with harmony and justice, till each mind listens to its spiritual wisdom. It has been promised that when our own mind listens to its true promptings and acts them out, almost in the twinkling of an eye, the mind of the whole world will listen and act wisely. For there is but one mind, and if one moves, all move. What one thinks and lives, all must think and live. This is true only of spiritual promptings. We cannot predicate anything of imaginary promptings: they seem to act, but do nothing. There really is but one power. That is Spirit. "There is none beside me."

June 4th teaches that sometimes when the spiritual nature is addressed for the purpose of making health manifest, the old diseases fight

with fresh determination to show themselves realities. And that when the spiritual nature is
addressed with the expectation of divine goodness
manifesting in the conduct, the old habits come
out like an army of Cossacks to make themselves
conquerors. And that when spiritual mind is spoken to, that it may stand forth satisfied with the
bounty of God, poverty comes with her shabby
flags and hunger pinches to claim the right of way
on this earth. Then the words of the heart and lips
must hug closer and closer to the truth of God.

That which is true of God concerning whole-
ness, goodness, ownership, is true of each of us
without exception. Nothing else or less is true.
Therefore, *"hold fast the form of sound words"* (II
Timothy 1:13). For all who hold on through the
period when evil seems to run riot as disease,
temptation, or poverty.

"The future hides in it gladness, not sorrow.

We press still through,

Naught that abides in it daunting us.

Onward!"

June 11th calls the physical body by beautiful
names; makes it the song of the Spirit in truth;
explains that the Spirit is hidden by a veil of de-
caying, changeable flesh, when we forget that it is
in truth all eternal, unalterable Spirit, not physical at all; teaches us at all times, waking or
sleeping, to keep singing in our minds, "I AM
Spirit, I AM Life, I AM Light, I AM Free," till we

have returned to the home from which we came out. God is our home. *"The Spirit shall return unto God who gave it"* (Ecclesiastes 12:7).

June 18th tears up the old notion the world has wrapped around itself that God is very slow to help, very slow to hear, very slow to perform. *"I will be a swift witness"* (Malachi 3:5), says this lesson. *"The Lord whom ye seek shall suddenly come"* (Malachi 3:1).

All that God is ever going to do He has already done. His work is finished. We hold a great banner up before our faces that declares "the bad comes swiftly; the good comes slowly. God is going to do something He has not done yet." Our arms are very tired and our hearts are very faint with holding up that banner. The time has come to put it down and rest. God is rest and quick reward. Nobody is too bad to put down that banner and fold himself around with the love of God. Nobody is too old to put down that flag and fold himself around with the life of God. Nobody is too poor to let go of that idea and be fed and clothed with the rich kindness of God.

This Sunday lesson, being a review, we are able to touch upon many points bearing on, but not much brought out in, regular lessons. Some one shining dart from the hearth fires of spiritual doctrine must pierce each heart as these 12 Bible lessons show you their purposes.

Inter-Ocean Newspaper, June 25, 1893

Notes

Other Books by Emma Curtis Hopkins

- *Class Lessons of 1888 (WiseWoman Press)*
- *Bible Interpretations (WiseWoman Press)*
- *Esoteric Philosophy in Spiritual Science (WiseWoman Press)*
- *Genesis Series*
- *High Mysticism (WiseWoman Press)*
- *Self Treatments with Radiant I Am (WiseWoman Press)*
- *The Gospel Series (WiseWoman Press)*
- *Judgment Series in Spiritual Science (WiseWoman Press)*
- *Drops of Gold (WiseWoman Press)*
- *Resume (WiseWoman Press)*
- *Scientific Christian Mental Practice (DeVorss)*

Books about Emma Curtis Hopkins and her teachings

- *Emma Curtis Hopkins, Forgotten Founder of New Thought –* *Gail Harley*
- *Unveiling Your Hidden Power: Emma Curtis Hopkins' Meta-physics for the 21st Century (also as a Workbook and as A Guide for Teachers) – Ruth L. Miller*
- *Power to Heal: Easy reading biography for all ages –Ruth Miller*

To find more of Emma's work, including some previously unpublished material, log on to:

www.emmacurtishopkins.com

WISEWOMAN PRESS

1408 NE 65th St
Vancouver, WA 98665
800.603.3005
www.wisewomanpress.com

Books Published by WiseWoman Press

By Emma Curtis Hopkins

- *Resume*
- *Gospel Series*
- *Class Lessons of 1888*
- *Self Treatments including Radiant I Am*
- *High Mysticism*
- *Esoteric Philosophy in Spiritual Science*
- *Drops of Gold Journal*
- *Judgment Series*
- *Bible Interpretations: Series I, II, III, IV, V, and VI*

By Ruth L. Miller

- *Unveiling Your Hidden Power: Emma Curtis Hopkins' Metaphysics for the 21st Century*
- *Coming into Freedom: Emily Cady's Lessons in Truth for the 21st Century*
- *150 Years of Healing: The Founders and Science of New Thought*
- *Power Beyond Magic: Ernest Holmes Biography*
- *Power to Heal: Emma Curtis Hopkins Biography*
- *The Power of Unity: Charles Fillmore Biography*
- *The Power of Mind: Phineas P. Quimby Biography*
- *Uncommon Prayer*
- *Spiritual Success*
- *Gracie's Adventures with God (Children's book)*

Watch our website for release dates and order information! - www.wisewomanpress.com

List of
Bible Interpretation Series
with date from 1st to 14th Series.

This list is complete through the fourteenth Series. Emma produced at least thirty Series of Bible Interpretations.

She followed the Bible Passages provided by the International Committee of Clerics who produced the Bible Quotations for each year's use in churches all over the world.

Emma used these for her column of Bible Interpretations in both the Christian Science Magazine, at her Seminary and in the Chicago Inter-Ocean Newspaper.

First Series

Second Series

Third Series

Fourth Series

Fifth Series

Sixth Series

Seventh Series

Eighth Series

Ninth Series

July 2 - September 27, 1893

Lesson 1	Secret of all Power	July 2nd
Acts 16: 6-15	The Ancient Chinese Doctrine of Taoism	
	Manifesting of God Powers	
	Paul, Timothy, and Silas	
	Is Fulfilling as Prophecy	
	The Inner Prompting.	
	Good Taoist Never Depressed	
Lesson 2	The Flame of Spiritual Verity	July 9th
Acts 16:18	Cause of Contention	
	Delusive Doctrines	
	Paul's History	
	Keynotes	
	Doctrine Not New	
Lesson 3	Healing Energy Gifts	July 16th
Acts 18:19-21	How Paul Healed	
	To Work Miracles	
	Paul Worked in Fear	
	Shakespeare's Idea of Loss	
	Endurance the Sign of Power	
Lesson 4	Be Still My Soul	July 23rd
Acts 17:16-24	Seeing Is Believing	
	Paul Stood Alone	
	Lessons for the Athenians	
	All Under His Power	
	Freedom of Spirit	
Lesson 5	(Missing) Acts 18:1-11	July 30th
Lesson 6	Missing No Lesson *	August 6th
Lesson 7	The Comforter is the Holy Ghost	August 13th
Acts 20	Requisite for an Orator	
	What is a Myth	
	Two Important Points	
	Truth of the Gospel	
	Kingdom of the Spirit	
	Do Not Believe in Weakness	

Tenth Series

Eleventh Series

147

Twelfth Series

April 1 – June 24, 1894

149

Thirteenth Series

151

Fourteenth Series